TWO'S COMPANY

A COOKBOOK FOR COUPLES

BEV BENNETT

Barron's
Woodbury, New York • London • Toronto • Sydney

Photographic Credits
Color photographs by Matthew Klein
Food styling by Andrea Swenson
Photo styling by Linda Cheverton

We are grateful to the following for supplying
props for the photos: china from Haviland &
Company, New York City; silver from Buccellati,
New York City; flowers by Very Special Flowers,
New York City; antique table from Pierre Deux,
New York City.

Book design by Milton Glaser, Inc.

All inquiries should be addressed to:
Barron's Educational Series, Inc.
113 Crossways Park Drive
Woodbury, New York 11797

International Standard Book No. 0–8120–5596–9

Library of Congress Cataloging No. 85–11274

**Library of Congress Cataloging-in-Publication
Data**
Bennett, Bev.
  Two's company.

  Includes index.
  1. Cookery for one.   2. Cookery for two.
I. Title.
TX652.B395   1985   641.5′61   85–11274
ISBN 0–8120–5596–9

PRINTED IN THE UNITED STATES OF
AMERICA
5 6 7 8   9 8 7 6 5 4 3 2 1

CONTENTS

ACKNOWLEDGMENTS

Thanks to Kim Upton for her support and encouragement, to Jean Barrett for her wine suggestions, to Virginia Motan for her recommendations, and to Carole Berglie for her generosity and wisdom.

DEDICATION

To Linn and Benji, who prove that three's not a crowd.

INTRODUCTION

IF you purchased this book you're part of a cooking revolution. You're one of a growing number of one- or two-person households with special shopping and cooking concerns. Whatever your family arrangements, you're likely to eat alone occasionally, and more often share a meal with one other person than with a full table.

Forget what you've imagined about Mom, Dad, and the kids sitting down together to dinner. That happens in a minority of homes. (According to the Census Bureau, 31.5 percent of U.S. households in 1983 consisted of two persons and 22.9 percent were singles, a total of about 54 percent.) For most people this is a new situation and requires a new way of cooking.

While the food industry is catching up to this revolution and offering products and ingredients in smaller packages, singles and twosomes are often at a loss on how to put a meal together.

Most recipes still yield four to six servings, meaning endless leftovers. Cooking for one or two isn't a matter of taking your favorite recipe and putting less on the table, despite what the late comedienne Gracie Allen said:

"When mother had to get dinner for eight, she'd just make enough for sixteen and only serve half."*

What's needed, of course, is a cookbook like this, that takes into account the desire to nourish yourself, body and spirit. Cooking for one or two is an art you can excel in.

Cooking for two is intimate. It's a time for sharing, for exchanging ideas, for experimenting with new recipes, and for enjoying the results together.

*From Maria Polushkin Robbins', *The Cook's Quotation Book*, Penguin.

Cooking for one is no less pleasurable. It is independent. It is never having to say you're sorry for the garlicky aroma in the kitchen. It's being able to shake a few extra red pepper flakes into the Scallops with Angel-Hair Pasta without setting off other peoples' heat alarms. It's being able to hoard a stack of chocolate cookies to ration out on a dreary day.

It's being able to proceed at your own pace, rather than that of a ravenous group. One evening you might enjoy making pasta from scratch; another time you might prefer a quick-cooking dish with prepared pasta. It's your choice. You can cater to your tastes.

Until now it seemed easier to pick up a frozen dinner on the way home; or, if you're part of a twosome, to go to still another restaurant for dinner. Instead, you can have easy, elegant meals, and save time and money, using these recipes.

This book has all the information and recipes you'll need to prepare wholesome and delicious meals for yourself. It has been created with the single or twosome in mind.

The recipes are planned around the many readily available items for one or two. Foods are seasoned with the right proportion of herbs and spices to other ingredients.

Each entree recipe has an accompanying salad, vegetable, or starch. There's no guesswork about putting a meal together. However, you may find other dishes in the book that work as well and give the main course a new touch. Select desserts according to the season and your appetite.

Most of the dishes take an hour or less to prepare at a leisurely pace. Frozen dinners, which are expensive, often take more time to cook.

The soups and stews in the book require a couple of hours, but then a soup marathon on a Sunday afternoon means an instant meal Monday night. Soups and stews improve in taste with a day's wait.

Though the majority of recipes are for two (a few soups and stews, and several desserts that keep well have larger yields), information on halving the ingredients is given when feasible.

I'd recommend singles make the full two-serving portions. In the hour it takes to make one meal, a single will have two. I prefer to freeze leftovers for a quick lunch or dinner a few weeks later, rather than face the same food two consecutive days.

Mother Nature is very sympathetic to the needs of the single. It's easier to get fresh than canned or frozen produce in small portions (try buying four frozen asparagus spears or one canned artichoke bottom), so that's what I emphasize. When purchased in season, fresh ingredients are the most economical and most nourishing choice.

The book's chapters are divided by months, so you'll have recipes for fresh artichokes in April when they are abundant, and corn in July and August. Even the recipes in the special-occasions section take seasonal items into account.

Some supermarkets pre-wrap fresh produce in large packages. Ask a store employee to rewrap one onion, one or two potatoes, or a handful of asparagus. You have the right to buy just the amount you need. Many meat, poultry, and fish items seem designed for one or two: a pork chop, a chicken breast, a trout, a fish fillet, a Rock Cornish hen, or a duck.

If you buy more meat than you need, the best alternative is to freeze the leftovers. The extra raw meat or poultry (make sure it wasn't previously frozen by the store) should be frozen as soon as you bring it home. Wrap it in single-serving, airtight packages. Label each package with the ingredient and date, and freeze. If the product was frozen and thawed, cook the entire amount, not just the portion you're ready to eat, and freeze the cooked leftovers. Don't keep raw beef in the refrigerator more than three days; raw ground beef or poultry more than two days. Raw or cooked beef, pork, and poultry can be frozen at least a month.

Although I emphasize fresh ingredients, I do use some convenience products and suspect that you will, too. Choose only those which truly save time and can be stored for long periods.

Some of my favorites include tomato paste in a tube, which stays fresh longer than canned tomato paste when opened; caviar paste in a tube, for flavoring salad dressings or simply as a spread; Minor's bases*, to use for stocks and broths; frozen wonton wrappers which double as ravioli skins, and frozen puff pastry.

I consider herbs a convenience and also an ingredient worth some discussion. A good pinch of oregano can transform a bland chicken breast dish into an aromatic delight. A rosemary sprig tucked into a casserole of baked potatoes and garlic results in a heady dish. Herbs make an instant impression.

If you love herbs as I do, you may want to keep plants such as rosemary, marjoram, thyme, and oregano around the house. Just pinch off what you need and you've got convenient flavorings.

* Minor's bases are concentrated pastes in a variety of flavors. They are sold in the refrigerated cases in gourmet and some grocery stores. For more information on availability write to L. J. Minor Corp., Cleveland, Ohio 44115.

Even if you don't grow herbs you should be able to find fresh Italian and curly parsley, dill, and coriander in stores the year round. Mint, basil, and rosemary are becoming more popular winter herbs.

I don't recommend substituting dried for fresh basil. I limit basil recipes to the summer months when it is readily available. Likewise, I wouldn't use dried parsley or dill (and I've never seen dried coriander leaves), as they are relatively tasteless.

Conversely, I prefer the taste of dried to fresh oregano for most dishes. It is more pungent and makes more of an impact in cooked foods. When I want a light taste of oregano, as in the Panzanella on page 118, I'll use the fresh herb.

With the exceptions of basil, dill, coriander, and parsley, recipes include measurements for both fresh and dried herbs. The general rule is to use one third to one half as much dried as fresh herb, but it is impossible to be exact. Dried herbs vary so much in intensity among the brands, or even among bottles that were packed on different dates. Start by using one third as much of the dried herb; you can always add more to your taste. You'll find that dried herbs have more flavor if they are crushed and soaked in a little warm water for 10 minutes before using.

Never keep dried herbs in direct light or heat, and especially not over the stove. I find that herbs and spices keep longer in the refrigerator.

Since singles or twosomes often have kitchens that are better suited for Barbie dolls than human-sized cooks (let's face it, no one's kitchen is ever big enough), every inch counts. Here is a list of items I find useful followed by those I can easily do without. Add according to your individual needs (but if you absolutely need a 2-foot electric potato peeler you aren't taking this seriously).

My kitchen includes:

■ A colorful place mat and matching napkin (you may prefer a beautiful wooden dinner tray). I also have a place setting with matching plate, bowl, cup, and saucer and good tableware. There's no excuse for eating over the kitchen sink.

■ A 2-cup oven-proof casserole dish. I use this for custards, crustless quiche, casseroles, and some meat loaves.

■ A 1-quart oven-proof casserole dish for pot pies, cobblers, and baked fruit dishes. This doubles as a salad bowl or vegetable serving bowl.

■ A 1-quart pot or saucepan with a lid. Cook oatmeal, rice, or an egg in this. Reheat small amounts of soup or stew quickly.

■ A 3-quart heavy-bottomed pot with a lid to handle bigger jobs, such as small quantities of soups or stews. Use it with the 1-quart pot for a double boiler.

■ A 5-quart pot or Dutch oven. It should have a wide cooking surface, a lid, and a heavy bottom. Use it for the larger quantity stews and soups that require long, slow simmering. Choose the best quality affordable.

■ A 7- or 8-inch skillet for frying eggs or sautéing small amounts of onions or other vegetables.

■ A 10- to 12-inch heavy-bottomed skillet for cooking a variety of vegetables for a ratatouille, for frying chicken, or making hamburgers or pancakes.

■ Mini loaf pans for individual breads or meat loaf.

■ One large jelly-roll pan, 10-by-15 inches, that will double as a cookie sheet (since I don't include that on my essentials list). Invest in a good-quality one that won't buckle on sustained use.

■ Muffin tins—those who don't like muffins as much as I do can skip these.

■ A 9-inch square pan for brownies, small batches of cookies, or for holding a smaller cake pan.

■ An 8- or 9-inch springform pan, only for those who love cheesecake as much as I do.

■ One 8-inch round cake pan.

■ An open-mesh cooling rack for cooling cakes, or roasting chicken, or keeping meat away from the drippings. Place the meat or poultry on the rack over the jelly-roll pan and roast.

■ A 7-inch tart ring with a removable bottom. This size yields a quiche or pie that's just right for two. Most good cookware stores should carry this.

■ The usual assortment of knives (don't get cheap here; it will be more costly eventually), measuring spoons and cups, personally useful gadgets, and tableware.

It's also nice to have:

■ A good coffee maker. Choose one that will make 2 cups at a time, the equivalent of one mug.

■ A hand-held mixer for cake batters, whipped cream, and beaten egg whites.

■ A blender or food processor.

I never use a toaster (when I crave crunchy bread I put a slice in a 400-degree oven for five minutes), an electric can opener, an electric knife, or an automatic air freshener (when I cook I want people to know it).

Here are some additional notes for following the recipes:

■ All butter is unsalted. Even if this is an ingredient you rarely use, buy it by the pound, which is cheaper than by the stick. However, choose a package divided into four sticks instead of in a block. Keep one stick of butter in the refrigerator and the rest in the freezer.

■ When preparing one of the pasta dishes in the book, fill a large pot with water and a tablespoon of vegetable or olive oil to prevent the pasta from sticking (some say this is unnecessary) and start heating it while you prepare the sauce. Don't cook the pasta, though, until the sauce is almost finished. The sauce will wait; pasta won't. Fresh pasta is done when it is tender; dried pasta is done when it still has some firmness in the center. Never rinse the pasta before serving.

■ Several recipes call for cooking chicken or seafood in wine or a combination of white wine and water. This is best done in a nonaluminum pot (aluminum is harmless but can discolor food cooked in white wine). When making chicken for salad I cook the chicken in wine and water and discard the cooking liquid. For Chicken Pot Pie, which also uses the broth, I prefer cooking the chicken in chicken broth (either homemade or commercially pre-pared).

■ Unless otherwise specified, eggs are large size.

■ The meat for the Skewered Rib Roast is Prime grade. For all other meat recipes buy Choice grade. It is less expensive and less fatty.

CHAPTER

1

Though there's still an abundance of summer tomatoes, squash, corn, plums, melons, and grapes on the market, supplies dwindle in September. Take advantage of lush, soft fruits and vegetables now.

Prepare Spinach and Shrimp with Rice and Celery Vinaigrette as a salad course. The rich, creamy shrimp dish goes well with the piquant, crisp salad.

Meaty Ratatouille, made with onions, zucchini, tomatoes, garlic, eggplant, and herbs is a hearty dish that is marvelous for tail-gate picnics. It keeps well, can be frozen, and tastes just as delicious when reheated. Match it with a rustic Cheese-Pepper Bread.

A fresh and zesty alternative to the classic quiche is Goat Cheese Tart, using plum tomatoes, red onions, Niçoise olives, and goat cheese. The tart goes very well with a sharp-flavored Zucchini-Yogurt Soup. Since both could be served cold, the menu is another picnic, or office lunch, possibility.

Frozen puff pastry is a quick alternative to yeast dough when you'd like a pizza for one or two. Make a side dish that's just as simple. Flavor carrots with orange marmalade and allspice.

SEPTEMBER

SPINACH AND SHRIMP

INGREDIENTS

5 to 6 ounces fresh spinach
3 tablespoons butter
8 ounces large, raw shrimp,
   shelled and deveined
2 tablespoons brandy
¼ teaspoon ground nutmeg
½ cup heavy cream
Salt and freshly ground white
   pepper to taste

1 Wash spinach and remove stems. Roll up leaves and slice into ½-inch strips. Place in steamer over boiling water. Cover and steam for 2 minutes. Drain and set aside.

2 Meanwhile, melt 2 tablespoons butter in large skillet. Add shrimp and cook just until pink. Remove and keep warm. Add brandy and stir up any browned bits on bottom of skillet. Cook 1 minute to remove raw brandy taste.

3 Add nutmeg and cream and cook over medium heat, stirring occasionally until mixture is slightly thickened. This only takes a few minutes. Add shrimp, spinach, salt, and white pepper. Cook over low heat, stirring to heat through. Remove from heat and swirl in remaining tablespoon butter. Serve immediately.

NOTE *This dish is also excellent using mussels in place of the shrimp. Purchase 1 pound of mussels. Clean, scraping off any dirt from the shells and pulling off beards with a sharp knife. Place mussels in a bowl with cold water to cover. Stir in a tablespoon or two of cornmeal and set aside 1 hour. Discard water mixture. Rinse mussels under cold running water and discard any that won't close.*

Heat 1 cup dry white wine in a medium pot. When it comes to the boil, add 2 bay leaves and the mussels. Cover and cook over medium heat 3 to 4 minutes, shaking pot. Shells should open; discard any that don't. Set aside until cool enough to handle, then pluck meat from the shells and set aside. Discard shells.

Prepare the dish according to the recipe, substituting mussels for the shrimp, but just heat the mussels through; don't allow to cook again or the meat will be tough.

RICE AND CELERY VINAIGRETTE

INGREDIENTS

½ cup rice
1 cup water
4 teaspoons white wine
    vinegar
1 tablespoon olive oil
2½ tablespoons vegetable oil
½ to ¾ teaspoon fresh,
    minced, or ¼ teaspoon
    crushed, dried thyme

¼ teaspoon freshly ground
    white pepper
½ cup coarsely chopped
    pimiento-stuffed olives
1 small celery stalk, diced
Salt to taste

1 Combine rice and water in a small pot. Bring to a boil. Reduce heat and cover pot. Simmer 12 to 15 minutes, until rice is just tender and water is absorbed. Set rice aside until it is lukewarm.

2 Spoon the rice into a serving bowl. Whisk together the vinegar, olive oil, vegetable oil, thyme, and white pepper. Pour over the rice. Add the olives and celery pieces. Toss the mixture gently, but well. Set aside at room temperature for 30 minutes for flavors to blend. Season with salt just before serving.

NOTE *For a more colorful and nourishing salad, add 1 peeled, seeded, and diced tomato when stirring in the olives and celery.*

To peel a tomato, bring a small pot of water to a boil. Spear the tomato with a fork and submerge in the water for 30 seconds. Remove. Use a paring knife to prick the skin; it should slip off easily.

To seed a tomato, cut in half crosswise and squeeze the halves over the sink so the seeds fall out or scoop out the seeds from their cavities using your fingers.

MEATY RATATOUILLE

INGREDIENTS

1 small eggplant (about 1 pound)
Salt to taste
1/2 pound hot or mild Italian sausage, casings removed
4 tablespoons olive oil
1 medium onion, peeled and chopped
1 small zucchini, cut in half lengthwise, then into 1/4-inch pieces

1 large clove garlic, minced
2 medium tomatoes, cored and chopped
1/2 teaspoon crushed, dried oregano
1/4 to 1/2 teaspoon fresh, minced, or 1/8 teaspoon crushed, dried marjoram
Freshly ground black pepper to taste

1 Cut eggplant into 1-inch-thick slices. Do not peel. Salt the slices and set aside for 1 hour.

2 Meanwhile, break the sausage into small pieces. Brown in a large skillet. Spoon out the sausage pieces and set aside. Discard any fat in the skillet.

3 Heat 2 tablespoons of the olive oil in the skillet. Add onions and sauté 5 minutes.

4 When eggplant has completed the salting, pat off any salt and bitter liquids that accumulate on the slices. Cube the eggplant and add to the skillet. Sauté another 5 minutes, stirring occasionally. Add remaining 2 tablespoons oil. Add zucchini and garlic. Cover the skillet and cook over low heat 15 minutes, stirring once or twice. Add tomato pieces, reserved sausage, oregano, marjoram, and pepper. Simmer, covered, 10 minutes. Taste and season with salt if necessary. Serve hot.

NOTE *Ratatouille always tastes better if it has a day to rest. If possible make this dish a day in advance.*

OPPOSITE: Meaty Ratatouille with Cheese-Pepper Bread (page 5).

FOLLOWING PHOTO: Tacos for Two (page 12).

CHEESE-PEPPER BREAD

INGREDIENTS

1 package active dry yeast
1 teaspoon sugar
1 cup warm water, divided
2 tablespoons vegetable oil
2½ to 2¾ cups all-purpose flour

1 teaspoon salt
1½ teaspoons freshly ground
 black pepper
1 cup grated Swiss cheese
Cornmeal

1 Sprinkle yeast over sugar and ¼ cup warm water in a small bowl. Stir and set aside for 10 minutes, until yeast dissolves and becomes foamy. Stir oil into yeast mixture.

2 In the bowl of a heavy-duty mixer fitted with a dough hook, combine 2¼ cups flour and the salt. Stir to mix. Stir in the yeast mixture, pepper, cheese, and the remaining ¾ cup warm water. Turn the mixer on to knead the dough; knead about 5 minutes, gradually adding more flour, by the tablespoon to get a dough that is elastic, but still slightly sticky.

3 Place the dough in a greased bowl, turning to grease all sides. Cover the bowl with a towel and set aside in a warm place for 1 hour.

4 Turn dough out onto a floured board and punch down. Divide into 2 pieces. Roll into 2 loaves, each about 8 inches long.

5 Sprinkle a cookie sheet with a little cornmeal. Place the breads on the cookie sheet and cover with a towel. Set aside in a warm place for 30 minutes.

6 Preheat oven to 375 degrees.

7 Bake the breads for 35 minutes, or until golden. Allow to cool on cookie sheet for about 30 minutes, then remove to rack and cool completely.

PHOTO OPPOSITE PAGE 4. MAKES 2 SMALL LOAVES

NOTE *To make this bread by hand, place 2 cups of flour and the 1 teaspoon salt in a large mixing bowl. Stir in the yeast mixture, pepper, cheese, and remaining ¾ cup warm water. Add a little more flour, if necessary to get a dough that is firm enough to knead. Turn the dough out onto a floured board and knead about 10 minutes, until elastic, but not dry. Add more flour to the board as necessary.*

GOAT CHEESE TART

INGREDIENTS

1 whole-wheat crust (recipe
  follows)
2 plum tomatoes, peeled,
  seeded, and thinly sliced
1 small red onion, peeled and
  thinly sliced

2 tablespoons olive oil
$1/2$ cup pitted Niçoise olives
$1/2$ teaspoon dried oregano
1 cup goat cheese

1 Preheat oven to 425 degrees.

2 Prepare whole-wheat crust. Bake for 5 minutes. Remove from the oven and set aside to cool.

3 Set tomato slices on a plate to drain. Separate onion slices into rings and sauté in 1 tablespoon oil over low heat for 7 to 10 minutes, until tender and lightly browned.

4 Arrange tomato slices on the bottom of the pie shell. Spread sautéed onions on top. Scatter olives over onions. Sprinkle on $1/4$ teaspoon oregano. Crumble cheese and sprinkle over the tart. Top with remaining $1/4$ teaspoon oregano and drizzle on remaining 1 tablespoon oil. Bake for 12 to 15 minutes, or until ingredients are thoroughly heated. Serve hot or tepid.

NOTE *This tart is a delicious, low-fat alternative to the usual cream and egg-laden quiche. But because it doesn't use eggs or cream as binders as a quiche does, it is a little more crumbly. For picnics leave the tart in the tart pan.*

WHOLE-WHEAT CRUST

INGREDIENTS

¼ cup all-purpose flour
¼ cup whole-wheat flour
Dash of salt
2 tablespoons cold butter, cut
* in small pieces*

1 tablespoon vegetable
* shortening*
1 egg yolk beaten with
* 1 tablespoon water*

1 Mix together all-purpose flour, whole-wheat flour, and salt in a bowl. Cut in butter pieces and shortening until mixture resembles coarse meal. Pour in egg yolk and water and stir with a fork until the mixture holds together. Dough should be very soft but not sticky. Wrap dough in plastic wrap and refrigerate 30 minutes.

2 Roll out dough on floured surface, using a floured rolling pin to a 10-inch circle. Gently ease into a 7-inch tart pan with a removable bottom.

NOTE *I prefer the nutty flavor that the whole-wheat flour imparts to this crust. However, all-purpose flour could be used alone; increase the all-purpose flour to ½ cup.*

As an added convenience you can make this crust in advance and freeze it. Bake for 10 minutes instead of 5, then allow it to cool completely. Remove from the tart pan, wrap in foil, and freeze for up to 6 months. To make the tart, defrost the crust, prepare the filling, and bake as usual.

ZUCCHINI-YOGURT SOUP

INGREDIENTS

1 tablespoon butter
2 small or 1 large shallot to
  yield 2 tablespoons minced
3/4 pound zucchini, sliced
1½ cups chicken broth
2 tablespoons fresh, minced
  Italian parsley
1 teaspoon minced lemon
  rind

Salt and freshly ground white
  pepper to taste
½ cup plain yogurt
A few parsley leaves for
  garnish

1 Melt butter in a medium pot. Add shallot and sauté over low heat for 5 minutes, stirring occasionally. Add zucchini and cook 5 more minutes. Add broth and parsley and bring to a simmer. Cover and cook 15 minutes or until zucchini is tender. Cool.

2 Place mixture in a food processor fitted with a steel blade or put through a food mill and puree until smooth. Pour into a serving bowl. Add lemon rind, salt, and white pepper. Whisk in yogurt. Chill for 1 to 3 hours. Serve with a parsley garnish.

NOTE *For a light entree, cook a half of a chicken breast, using the 1½ cups chicken broth called for in the zucchini-yogurt soup. Reserve the broth, cool it, and use it for the zucchini mixture. Tear the chicken meat from the bones and add to the soup just before it is chilled.*

PIZZA PUFF

INGREDIENTS

*4 frozen puff pastry patty
  shells*
2 tablespoons butter
½ cup chopped onion
1 cup sliced mushrooms
1 can (8 ounces) tomato sauce
¼ teaspoon dried oregano
1 small clove garlic, minced
2 tablespoons dry red wine
Dash cayenne pepper

*Salt and freshly ground white
  pepper to taste*
1 teaspoon minced fresh parsley
*1 cup shredded mozzarella
  cheese*
*2 ounces (about ½ cup)
  chopped pepperoni, ham,
  or salami (optional)*
*1 egg white mixed with
  1 teaspoon water*

1 Preheat oven to 375 degrees.

2 Thaw patty shells and set aside while preparing filling. Melt butter in small skillet. Sauté onion and mushrooms 5 minutes until onions are transparent, but not brown. Add tomato sauce, oregano, garlic, wine, cayenne, salt, white pepper, and parsley. Simmer 10 minutes. Taste and adjust seasonings as necessary.

3 On lightly floured board, roll out the patty shells into thin circles about 6 inches in diameter. All circles should be the same size and shape, but don't take too long at it or the dough will become sticky.

4 Divide the tomato sauce mixture between 2 of the patty shells, keeping the sauce to within 1 inch of the edge. Divide the cheese between the circles. If using meat, sprinkle it over the cheese.

5 Brush the pastry borders with egg white. Top one at a time with remaining circles. Press edges with fork tines to seal. Brush tops of pizzas with remaining egg white. Make a slash in each pizza top for steam to escape.

6 Place pizzas on greased pan and bake for 30 minutes or until crusts are puffed and lightly browned. Remove from oven and serve immediately.

NOTE *Recipe can be halved.*

MARMALADE CARROTS

INGREDIENTS

2 medium carrots
¼ cup water
1½ tablespoons butter
1½ to 2 tablespoons orange
   marmalade
¼ teaspoon ground allspice
Salt to taste

1 Peel carrots and slice ¼ inch thick, to yield about 1½ cups. Place in a small pot with water and 1 tablespoon butter. Simmer, covered, 15 to 20 minutes, until tender.

2 Remove the cover from the pot, turn the heat to high, and cook off the remaining water. Remove the pot from heat. Stir in the remaining butter, orange marmalade, allspice, and salt.

NOTE *Recipe can be halved.*
   To vary this dish, cook the carrots according to the directions. Then puree them in a blender or food processor fitted with a steel blade. Stir in the remaining ½ tablespoon butter, orange marmalade, allspice, and salt.
   The combination of orange marmalade and allspice is also nice with sweet potatoes. Slice a medium-size sweet potato and boil in water to cover until tender, about 20 minutes. Then proceed as for the carrots.

CHAPTER

2

There's a real autumn influence in this month's menus. Among the new things to look for are cranberries, persimmons, pomegranates, and hard-shell squash. Include more hot dishes on the menu. It's a month for energizing food.

Start with Tacos for Two. If it's impossible to keep the lettuce, tomato, cheese, and meat together, don't worry. The fun of tacos is that they're messy. Add a little heat with Hot Stuff, a quick salsa.

Stock up on cranberries. They freeze very well and don't require thawing before using in a cooked product. Be sure to have enough for delicious Cranberry-Orange Pancakes. Round out the meal with Hot, Buttered Rummy Grapefruit and Spiced Apple Cider.

Hot and Sour Chicken Soup, a Thai specialty, has been adapted to use readily available ingredients. If you're fortunate enough to have a Thai market nearby, use the authentic lemon grass and lime leaves suggested in the recipe. Sweet and Sour Pepper Salad is an invention that is reminiscent of the relish-like salads in Thai restaurants.

The traditional Thai soups are clear broths, potently flavored. An all-American Cheese Soup by contrast is creamy and subtly seasoned. Put a little zest into the meal with Spaghetti Squash with Ginger-Tomato Sauce.

OCTOBER

TACOS FOR TWO

INGREDIENTS

1 very small onion, peeled
  and chopped
1 tablespoon vegetable oil
1/2 pound ground chuck
2 tablespoons tomato paste
1 1/2 teaspoons ground cumin
1/4 teaspoon salt
1/8 teaspoon freshly ground
  black pepper
Dash of ground nutmeg
1 teaspoon chili powder

4 to 5 taco shells
1 cup shredded lettuce
1 medium tomato, seeded
  and diced
1/2 cup grated Monterey Jack
  cheese or other mild white
  cheese
4 to 5 teaspoons chopped,
  canned jalapeño peppers
  (optional)
Hot Stuff (recipe follows)

1 Preheat the oven to 350 degrees.

2 In medium skillet, sauté onion in oil for 5 minutes, or until tender, but not browned. Add ground chuck and break up with a fork. Cook, stirring occasionally, until no pink remains in the meat, about 5 minutes.

3 Stir in the tomato paste, cumin, salt, pepper, nutmeg, and chili powder. Simmer 5 minutes.

4 Divide the meat mixture among the taco shells. Place on a cookie sheet and heat for 5 minutes. Remove. Top each taco with lettuce, tomato, and a sprinkling of cheese. For really hot tacos, sprinkle a teaspoon of chopped jalapeño peppers over each serving. Serve Hot Stuff, a quick salsa, on the side.

PHOTO OPPOSITE PAGE 5

HOT STUFF

INGREDIENTS

2 small jalapeño peppers
1 small shallot, peeled
1 cup canned seeded
    tomatoes, drained of juice
    (a 1-pound can of
    tomatoes); or fresh, seeded
    tomatoes, if the quality is
    good

1 teaspoon fresh, minced
    coriander (cilantro)
Salt and freshly ground black
    pepper to taste

1 Remove stems from jalapeño peppers. Cut in half lengthwise and remove seeds. In food processor fitted with steel blade, mince together pepper halves and shallot. Add tomatoes and process until mixture is blended, but still slightly chunky. Add coriander, salt, and pepper.

2 Spoon mixture out into a small bowl. Cover with plastic wrap and let sit 1 hour.

MAKES 1 CUP

NOTE *To do by hand, mince together jalapeño peppers and shallot. Finely chop tomatoes and add to pepper mixture along with coriander, salt, and pepper. This mixture keeps in the refrigerator up to one week. If you use a lot of salsa in your cooking, double or triple the recipe.*

CRANBERRY-ORANGE PANCAKES

INGREDIENTS

¾ cup milk
2 tablespoons butter, melted
1 egg
1 cup all-purpose flour
2 teaspoons baking powder
¼ cup sugar
½ teaspoon salt

*1 tablespoon grated orange
  rind*
*½ cup coarsely ground
  cranberries*

1 In a medium bowl, beat together the milk, melted butter, and egg. Onto that mixture dump the flour, baking powder, sugar, salt, and orange rind. Stir just to mix. Add the cranberries.

2 Generously grease and heat a pancake griddle. Pour out batter for 4 pancakes, each 4 to 5 inches in diameter. Cook until the batter looks bubbly on top, flip over and cook the underside. Repeat with remaining batter. Serve immediately.

MAKES 8 PANCAKES

NOTE *The recipe yield is too great for all but the most ardent pancake-loving singles, yet it is difficult to halve. Instead, I'd recommend singles make the full batter and cook all the pancakes. Stack half on a sheet of heavy-duty foil with plastic wrap between each pancake. Enclose the stack with the foil and freeze up to one month. To serve, remove as many pancakes as you like and heat in a skillet with a little butter or in a preheated 400-degree oven for 5 minutes.*

HOT, BUTTERED RUMMY GRAPEFRUIT

INGREDIENTS

1 grapefruit
2 tablespoons honey
2 teaspoons unsalted butter
1 tablespoon dark rum

1 Preheat oven to 550 degrees.

2 Cut grapefruit in half crosswise. Cut between the rind and the fruit segments, then, if desired, take a small knife and loosen fruit segments.

3 Place grapefruit halves in a small oven-proof dish. Drizzle each half with 1 tablespoon honey. Cut butter into thin slivers and top grapefruit halves with butter slivers. Carefully drizzle 1½ teaspoons rum into each grapefruit half. Broil for 6 to 8 minutes, watching carefully so grapefruit doesn't burn.

NOTE *If the thought of rum seems a bit overwhelming at 8 a.m., you can substitute rum extract. Combine ½ teaspoon rum extract with the honey and drizzle onto the grapefruit. Then add butter as directed.*
    To save a few minutes in the morning, you can prepare this dish the night before and allow the honey and rum to soak into the grapefruit. Then broil the fruit just before serving. Try this recipe whenever you have oranges that are too bitter. Serve 1 orange per person.

SPICED APPLE CIDER

INGREDIENTS

1½ cups apple juice
1 cinnamon stick
8 cloves
2 orange slices

1 Combine apple juice, cinnamon stick, and cloves in a small pot. Simmer, covered for 15 minutes.

2 Strain out the cinnamon and cloves. Divide the cider between 2 heat-proof mugs. Garnish each with an orange slice. Serve hot.

NOTE *To give this drink a little punch, add 1 ounce (2 tablespoons) of dark rum or brandy to each mug just before serving.*

Kim Upton prepares a knock-out drink that can take the chill out of the most blustery morning. Here's her recipe, pared down for two:

In a medium pot combine 1 cup dry red wine, 1 ounce (2 tablespoons) vodka, 1 ounce (2 tablespoons) brandy, 1 small cinnamon stick, ⅛ teaspoon cloves, 2 tablespoons raisins, 3 tablespoons blanched almonds, 1 tablespoon sugar, and 2 orange slices. Heat until hot, but do not boil. Turn off heat. Cover the pot and let sit for 15 minutes so the flavor develops. Then, reheat over low heat. Sieve into 2 mugs and garnish with 2 fresh orange slices. (If you'd like to keep the flavor, but omit the alcohol from this drink, just bring the liquids to a boil.)

HOT AND SOUR CHICKEN SOUP

INGREDIENTS

½ teaspoon chopped red chilies
½ teaspoon vegetable oil
2 cups chicken broth
2 pieces (2 to 3 inches each) lemon peel (see note)
1 piece (2 to 3 inches) lime peel (see note)
1 teaspoon nam pla *(see note)*

1 boneless chicken breast half, cut in strips or 1-inch cubes
1 cup Chinese cabbage, torn into bite-size pieces
½ cup fresh Chinese noodles
2 teaspoons fresh, minced coriander (cilantro)

1 Puree chilies and vegetable oil together. Set aside.

2 In a medium pot, combine chicken broth, lemon peel, lime peel, *nam pla*, and chili puree. Simmer 15 minutes. Add chicken and cabbage and simmer 10 more minutes.

3 Meanwhile, cook noodles in boiling water until tender, about 5 minutes. Drain well. Add noodles to the soup.

4 Spoon soup into 2 bowls. Garnish each with 1 teaspoon coriander.

SERVES 2 AS A FIRST COURSE; 1 AS A HEARTY ENTREE

NOTE *An authentic Thai hot and sour soup would use lemon grass instead of lemon peel and lime leaves in place of the lime peel. Both are hard to find. However, if you're fortunate enough to have these ingredients, substitute 1 stalk lemon grass, cut into 1-inch pieces and 2 lime leaves.* Nam pla, *the fish sauce, is usually available in Thai, Philippine, and Chinese grocery stores. Don't substitute soy sauce in this recipe.*

SWEET AND SOUR PEPPER SALAD

INGREDIENTS

1 celery stalk, diced
1 small red bell pepper, diced
2 tablespoons shallot-flavored
  white wine vinegar
1 tablespoon sugar
1 tablespoon fresh minced
  parsley
Salt and freshly ground white
  pepper to taste

1 Combine the celery and red pepper pieces in a small serving bowl and set aside.

2 In a small cup, stir together the vinegar and sugar until the sugar dissolves. Add the parsley. Pour over the celery and pepper and toss well.

3 Season lightly with salt and white pepper. Chill 1 hour.

NOTE *My favorite variation on this salad is as follows: Scrub and thinly slice 1 large cucumber. Place one layer of cucumber slices in a medium glass or ceramic bowl. Sprinkle with salt. Continue layering until all the cucumbers are used. Cover the dish with plastic wrap and place a weight on top. Refrigerate for several hours. Drain off any liquid. Rinse the cucumber slices to get rid of excess salt and place in a colander to drain. To serve, mix 2 tablespoons shallot-flavored white wine vinegar, 1 tablespoon sugar, 1 tablespoon fresh, minced chervil or parsley, and freshly ground white pepper to taste. Stir until sugar dissolves. Spoon cucumber slices into a serving bowl and add the vinegar mixture. Toss well. Chill 1 hour.*

CHEESE SOUP

INGREDIENTS

*1 small green bell pepper,
    diced*
1 shallot, peeled and diced
2 tablespoons unsalted butter
*1½ tablespoons all-purpose
    flour*
¾ cup hot chicken broth
¾ cup half-and-half or milk
*1 cup grated sharp Cheddar
    cheese*

Dash of hot pepper sauce
*Salt and freshly ground white
    pepper to taste*

1 Sauté pepper and shallot in butter in medium pot for 5 minutes. Pepper should still be slightly crisp. Stir in flour until mixture becomes thick and pasty.

2 Gradually add hot chicken broth, stirring constantly until mixture is smooth and thick. Then add half-and-half. Add Cheddar, a little at a time, adding more when the first batch is melted in. Add a dash of hot pepper sauce, salt, and white pepper. Serve immediately.

NOTE *This soup can be adapted to suit your tastes. You can substitute red bell peppers for the green ones; use scallions in place of shallots, and Swiss cheese for the Cheddar. It is important that you use a full-flavored cheese; anything less would result in a bland product.*

Since this soup reheats so well in a microwave oven, you may want to double the recipe and freeze extras in single-serving containers. Keep the soup in the freezer up to 6 months.

SPAGHETTI SQUASH WITH GINGER-TOMATO SAUCE

INGREDIENTS

1 pound spaghetti squash
1 shallot, peeled
1 piece (1 inch) gingerroot
2 tablespoons butter
1 can (1 pound) tomatoes
A pinch of sugar
¼ teaspoon ground nutmeg

Dash of salt
Freshly ground white pepper
  to taste

1 Preheat oven to 400 degrees.

2 Place squash on a cookie sheet. Puncture in several places with fork tines to allow steam to escape. Bake for 45 minutes, turning occasionally until fork-tender.

3 While squash is baking, mince together shallot and gingerroot. Sauté together in 1 tablespoon butter in a small skillet for 5 minutes. Drain tomatoes, discarding liquid. Coarsely chop tomatoes by hand or in food processor. Add to ginger mixture. Add sugar, nutmeg, salt, and white pepper. Simmer for 20 minutes. Remove from heat and stir in remaining butter.

4 To serve, remove squash from oven. Cut in half lengthwise. Remove seeds. Spoon sauce over each half and allow diners to scrape out the "spaghetti" strands with a fork. Serve hot.

OPPOSITE: Baby Artichokes with Capers and Shrimp (page 130).

FOLLOWING PHOTO: Oriental Noodle Salad (page 30).

N
O
V
E
M
B
E
R

CHAPTER

3

One definition of eternity is two people and a turkey. It's difficult to justify purchasing even a small bird for a one- or two-person household. However, many people feel Thanksgiving isn't celebrated without some turkey dish.

Two possible alternatives to a whole turkey are fresh turkey cuts and turkey parts available in small, convenient packages. Fix either as you like. There's an excellent recipe for Turkey Marsala using turkey breast cutlets on page 78. In addition, the Rock Cornish Hens with Fruited Cornbread Stuffing on page 128 is a perfect Thanksgiving dish.

If leftovers are a problem (even without buying any turkey many people find themselves the recipients of a little care package provided by friends or relatives), there are two different recipes—a satisfying Sautéed Turkey Sandwich and a Turkey Soup—to transform the extras into a fine meal. Serve the sandwich with Apple-Cranberry Sauce that's been simmered with rum. Whole Wheat Biscuits round out the soup meal.

Other dishes for November include a Sausage Sandwich, with an accompaniment of creamy Cabbage-Onion Slaw, and Allan Mallory's creation of Sautéed Calves' Liver with Bacon and Pecans served with an Oriental Noodle Salad.

OPPOSITE: Arroz con Pollo (page 46).

PRECEDING PHOTO: Soft-shelled Crabs with Tarragon Sauce (page 134).

SAUTÉED TURKEY SANDWICH

INGREDIENTS

2 slices whole wheat bread
Butter
6 ounces sliced, cooked
    turkey
1½ teaspoons butter
1½ teaspoons all-purpose
    flour
½ cup milk, heated
1 ounce sharp Cheddar
    cheese, crumbled

1 teaspoon prepared white
    horseradish or 1
    tablespoon mustard
Dash of crushed red pepper
    flakes
Salt and freshly ground white
    pepper to taste

1 Butter bread on both sides. Place bread in large skillet. Cover each bread slice with 3 ounces turkey. Sauté over medium heat 5 minutes to heat through. If necessary add a little butter to the skillet to prevent the bread from sticking.

2 Meanwhile, melt 1½ teaspoons butter in a small pot over low heat. Add flour and stir until smooth. Add milk, and whisk until mixture is smooth and thickened. Add crumbled cheese. Stir until melted. Stir in horseradish or mustard, red pepper flakes, salt, and white pepper.

3 To serve, ease turkey sandwiches onto 2 plates. Spoon sauce over each sandwich.

NOTE *You can buy a turkey breast and roast it using the leftover meat for this recipe, or you can sauté turkey cutlets. The recipe can be halved.*

APPLE-CRANBERRY SAUCE

INGREDIENTS

1 tart apple
4 tablespoons apple juice
  concentrate (not
  reconstituted), thawed if
  frozen
¼ to ½ teaspoon ground
  ginger
¼ teaspoon ground
  cinnamon

1 cup cranberries
2 tablespoons sugar
2 tablespoons dark rum

1 Peel apple. Core and slice into ¼-inch thick slices. Combine with apple juice concentrate in small pot. Cover and simmer 5 minutes.

2 Add ginger, cinnamon, cranberries, sugar, and rum. Simmer another 5 minutes, covered.

NOTE *Experiment, substituting a pear for the apple and pear juice for the apple juice. Try serving this as a simple dessert, and not just as a relish. A bowl of the sauce and some chewy macaroons are a heady combination.*
*   If you enjoy canning, make this sauce in large batches. Pack in sterilized canning jars and process in a boiling water bath (follow the directions in any standard canning book). Jars of Apple-Cranberry Sauce will make welcome gifts at Christmas time.*
*   The recipe can be halved; use a small apple, or half a large one.*

TURKEY SOUP

INGREDIENTS

*3 pounds raw turkey backs
    and necks and any scraps
    of meat*
*4 celery stalks, including
    leaves*
3 carrots
2 onions
6 peppercorns
2½ quarts cold water
3 tablespoons butter
*1 can (28 ounces) Italian
    plum tomatoes*

*1 package (10 ounces) frozen
    okra or equivalent amount
    of fresh okra or ½ pound
    fresh green beans, trimmed
    and cut into 1-inch lengths*
*Salt and freshly ground white
    pepper to taste*
¼ teaspoon cayenne pepper
Cooked white or brown rice

1 First prepare broth.

2 Cut or break turkey pieces into large chunks. Place in large pot. Add 2 celery stalks, broken into large chunks, 1 carrot, scraped, and 1 onion, peeled and quartered. Crush peppercorns and add to pot. Add water. Bring to a boil. Skim off foam. Reduce heat, partially cover pot and simmer for 2 hours. Skim off foam occasionally.

3 Strain out solids. Discard vegetables and peppercorn pieces. Pick turkey meat off the bones and refrigerate. There should be about 2 cups turkey meat. Refrigerate broth, about 3 to 4 hours so fat solidifies.

4 To prepare soup, skim fat off top of soup and discard. You should have about 7 or 8 cups broth. Place broth over high heat and boil down to 6 cups.

5 Meanwhile, melt butter in large skillet. Slice remaining 2 celery stalks (with leaves) into ½-inch-thick pieces. Scrape remaining 2 carrots and slice ½-inch-thick. Peel and chop remaining onion. Sauté celery, carrots, and onion in skillet over low heat for 10 minutes.

6 Drain liquid off tomatoes (freeze and save for a soup if desired). Break tomatoes into large chunks and add to vegetables. If using okra, slice 1 inch thick and add to vegetables; otherwise add green beans. Add about 1 teaspoon salt, along with white pepper and cayenne. Bring to a boil. Skim off foam. Reduce heat to simmer. Simmer 45 minutes to 1 hour. Stir in reserved turkey and heat through. Adjust seasonings to taste.

7 For each serving place ½ cup cooked rice in bottom of large soup bowl. Spoon in soup and vegetable mixture.

8 Freeze leftovers in small, plastic containers. Keeps about 6 months.

SERVES 12

NOTE *Turkey soup can also be made using the carcass of a roasted turkey, preferably with a good amount of meat left.*

WHOLE-WHEAT BISCUITS

INGREDIENTS

¼ cup all-purpose flour
¼ cup whole-wheat flour
½ teaspoon baking powder
½ teaspoon sugar
Dash of salt
2 tablespoons butter
3 tablespoons heavy cream,
   half-and-half or milk

1 Preheat oven to 400 degrees.

2 Sift together all-purpose and whole-wheat flours, baking powder, sugar, and salt. Cut butter into slivers, then cut into flour mixture until crumbly. Add cream, half-and-half, or milk and toss with a fork to form a dough that sticks together. Knead a few times in the bowl.

3 Turn dough out onto floured board. Roll out ½ inch thick. Cut with cookie cutters about 2½ to 3 inches in diameter to form 4 biscuits.

4 Place biscuits on ungreased cookie sheet, making sure biscuits just touch for soft-sided crusts, or are spaced apart for a crunchy crust. Bake for 20 minutes or until nicely browned.

MAKES 4 BISCUITS

NOTE *These biscuits don't keep well. Either eat them within a few hours of baking, or freeze the leftovers. Thaw them, then reheat in a preheated 400-degree oven for 5 minutes. Spread with butter and jam for a breakfast indulgence.*

SAUSAGE SANDWICHES

INGREDIENTS

2 tablespoons olive oil
1 medium onion, peeled and
    thinly sliced
1 medium green bell pepper,
    cored and thinly sliced into
    strips
1/2 pound hot Italian sausage,
    cut in half
1/4 cup dry red wine
1 can (8 ounces) tomato
    sauce
2 tablespoons tomato paste
1 teaspoon dried oregano
1 teaspoon fresh, minced
    parsley
2 toasted French rolls

1 Heat oil in a large skillet. Add onion and green pepper and sauté until tender and lightly browned, about 10 minutes. Add sausage and brown on all sides. Add red wine and simmer 5 minutes. Add tomato sauce, tomato paste, oregano, and parsley. Simmer, covered, 30 minutes, stirring occasionally.

2 Make a deep slash down the length of both rolls. Divide sausage mixture between rolls.

NOTE *Hot Italian sausage usually lives up to its billing. You can substitute sweet sausage for the hot variety. For a completely mild sandwich, omit the sausage. Brown 8 ounces of ground beef and combine with the onion and green pepper. Continue with the recipe, then add salt, pepper, and red pepper flakes to taste. What you'll have is an adult recipe for a sloppy Joe.*
This dish freezes well. Pack into single-serving containers and freeze for up to 6 months. Defrost in the refrigerator and reheat. It may be necessary to adjust the seasonings.

CABBAGE-SCALLION SLAW

INGREDIENTS

2 packed cups thinly sliced
    cabbage
2 rounded tablespoons white
    and green parts of scallion,
    minced (about 1 scallion)
¼ cup mayonnaise
¼ teaspoon freshly ground
    white pepper
Salt to taste

1 Combine cabbage and scallions in a bowl. Add mayonnaise, white pepper, and salt and stir well.

2 Chill 1 hour before serving if possible.

NOTE *This is a basic cole slaw recipe. Here are some ways to vary it.*
    Add one or all of the following: ½ cup slivered red bell pepper, 1 tablespoon minced parsley, ½ cup raw, shredded parsnip, 1 to 2 tablespoons of sour cream or plain yogurt.
    I've been restrained in my use of curry powder in these recipes since I love the combination of curry powder and mayonnaise and could overwhelm a cook with my insistence on it. However, a teaspoon of curry powder with 4 tablespoons of mayonnaise is a good blend for this cole slaw, giving it a slightly sweet, hot taste.
    Curry powder calls for another combination of ingredients. Omit the scallions and add one or all of the following: 1 small red apple, diced; 1 small onion, peeled and diced; ½ cup chopped walnuts; ½ cup seedless or seeded red grapes, halved.

ALLAN MALLORY'S SAUTÉED CALVES' LIVER WITH BACON AND PECANS

INGREDIENTS

½ pound calves' liver, sliced
  ½ inch thick
2 tablespoons butter
2 tablespoons chopped
  pecans
4 strips bacon
1 tablespoon vegetable oil
Salt and freshly ground black
  pepper to taste

1 Trim membranes from liver. Cut liver into 2 serving portions. Set aside.

2 Melt 1 tablespoon butter in large skillet. Sauté pecans for 5 minutes. Remove and set aside. Wipe out the pan.

3 In a second pan, cook the bacon until crisp. Meanwhile heat remaining tablespoon butter and oil in the large skillet over medium heat. Add liver and cook 2 to 3 minutes per side, until browned on the outside and pink inside.

4 To serve, place liver on 2 serving plates. Top each portion with half the pecans and 2 bacon strips. Season lightly with salt, if desired, and with pepper.

NOTE *Recipe can be halved.*

ORIENTAL NOODLE SALAD

INGREDIENTS

3 tablespoons vegetable oil
2 tablespoons sunflower seeds
1/4 cup minced chives
1 firmly packed cup torn
  salad savoy leaves (see
  note)
1 cup fresh Chinese noodles
1 1/2 teaspoons sesame oil
2 teaspoons rice wine vinegar

1 1/2 teaspoons light soy sauce
Salt and freshly ground white
  pepper to taste

1 Heat 1 tablespoon vegetable oil in a small skillet. Sauté sunflower seeds until lightly browned, 3 to 4 minutes. Remove from heat. Combine in a bowl with chives.

2 Steam salad savoy for 3 minutes. Drain well and add to sunflower seeds. Cook noodles in plenty of boiling water until tender, about 5 minutes. Drain well; cool until lukewarm and add to salad savoy.

3 Whisk together remaining 2 tablespoons vegetable oil, sesame oil, rice wine vinegar, light soy sauce, salt, if necessary, and a generous amount of freshly ground white pepper.

4 Pour over salad mixture and toss well. Set aside for one hour if possible for flavors to blend.

PHOTO 2 FOLLOWING PAGE 20

NOTE *Salad savoy is a beautiful vegetable with a flavor similar to cabbage. The ruffle-edged leaves come in purple, pink and green bands or in shades of green. If this vegetable isn't available substitute Chinese cabbage.*

DECEMBER

CHAPTER

4

This month it's nice to have some traditional dishes on hand as well as some new things that might be appropriate for easy entertaining.

Oyster stew, often served on Christmas or New Year's Eve, is extremely simple, yet very satisfying. Serve it any time during the holiday season. An excellent match for the stew is a Parmesan Ring. This crusty, light "bread" of eggs and cheese is an adaptation of gougere, served during the wine harvest season in Burgundy. This recipe uses milk in place of water for a more tender dough and Parmesan instead of Gruyère cheese. Tear off pieces from the ring and use them to sop up every bit of the rich oyster stew.

Borscht, another cold-weather favorite, is transformed into an attractive pink pasta. Garnish the platter with the essential dollop of sour cream. Follow the recipe for making the pasta from scratch, or buy prepared beet pasta. A pungent Spinach and Parsley Salad with Hot Anchovy Dressing completes the meal.

Bread strata, a comfort food from childhood, gets an adult look when pimientos, prosciutto, and Swiss cheese are layered in with the bread. Serve the Prosciutto, Pimiento, and Cheese Strata with Fruited Butternut Squash. The combination is nice for brunch, as well as for dinner.

Kim Upton, a dear friend and great Chinese cook, developed Spicy Sirloin With Brown Rice and a Straw Mushroom Soup for two.

OYSTER STEW

INGREDIENTS

2 cups half-and-half
1 bay leaf
¼ to ½ teaspoon fresh,
  minced thyme or ⅛
  teaspoon crushed, dried
  thyme
1 cup fresh raw oysters and a
  little of their liquor

Salt and freshly ground white
  pepper to taste
1 tablespoon butter

1 In a small pot, simmer half-and-half with bay leaf and thyme for 10 minutes. Keep just below the boil. Remove bay leaf.

2 Add oysters and their liquor. Simmer an additional 5 minutes, until oysters plump up. Season with salt and white pepper. Pour into 2 bowls. Add ½ tablespoon butter to each bowl and allow to melt in. Serve immediately.

NOTE *You should have no trouble finding fresh raw oysters this month.*
But if it seems impossible, don't be tempted to substitute canned ones. They have a metallic taste that will ruin the stew. Instead substitute one of the following: ½ pound bay scallops; ½ pound halibut, cut into 1-inch cubes; ½ pound sea scallops, cut into thirds.
To cook, simmer the half-and-half with the bay leaf and thyme for 10 minutes. Remove the bay leaf. Then add the scallops or fish and any fish juices that accumulate.
Simmer for 5 minutes, or until the fish or scallops are no longer translucent. Season with salt and pepper and add the pat of butter just before serving.

PARMESAN RING

INGREDIENTS

½ cup milk
¼ cup butter, cut into small
    pieces
½ cup all-purpose flour
2 eggs, at room temperature
1 cup grated Parmesan cheese
Dash of hot pepper sauce

Salt and freshly ground white
    pepper to taste
1 egg white

1 Preheat oven to 400 degrees.

2 Combine milk and butter in heavy-bottomed pot. Bring to a boil. Add flour all at once. Reduce heat to low and stir mixture vigorously until it is smooth and comes away from side of pan. Turn off heat and cool mixture 5 minutes.

3 Beat in eggs, one at a time, beating well after each addition until eggs are incorporated and mixture is smooth. Stir in ¾ cup cheese and a generous dash of hot pepper sauce. Season with salt (go easy—the cheese is salty) and white pepper.

4 Using a tablespoon, heap mixture onto greased and floured cookie sheet forming an 8-inch circle. Brush top of ring with egg white. Carefully sprinkle remaining cheese around top of ring. Don't allow cheese to drop onto cookie sheet or it will burn.

5 Bake ring for 10 minutes. Reduce oven temperature to 350 degrees and bake an additional 20 minutes. Turn off heat and allow ring to rest for 10 minutes. Remove from oven and serve hot or tepid.

BORSCHT PASTA

INGREDIENTS

1 large beet, trimmed of any
  leaves or stems if necessary
1 large egg
Salt
1 to 1¼ cups all-purpose
  flour
1 tablespoon vegetable oil
1 tablespoon unsalted butter
½ to ¾ cup sour cream

1 to 2 teaspoons grated
  orange rind
Dash of ground nutmeg
Freshly ground white pepper
  to taste

1 Cut beet in quarters and cook in boiling water to cover until tender, about 20 to 30 minutes. Drain and set aside to cool. Peel.

2 Place 1 beet quarter in a food processor fitted with a steel blade, and puree. There should be 2 rounded tablespoons beet puree; if not add a little more beet and puree. To the beet in the food processor add egg, a dash of salt, and 1 cup flour. Process until mixture forms a slightly sticky mass. Add 1 or 2 more tablespoons flour and process again until dough comes together into a ball. Remove and divide in 2. Wrap in plastic wrap and set aside for 15 to 30 minutes.

3 Roll half the dough at a time through a pasta machine, flouring lightly as needed with remaining flour. If using a hand-crank machine, stop just before the finest adjustment. Sheets of pasta should be about 1/16 inch thick. Let sheets dry 5 minutes, then cut by hand or machine into noodles about ¼ inch wide. If using an electric pasta machine, follow the directions.

4 Allow noodles to dry (drape them on a broomstick set across 2 chairs if necessary) and repeat noodle making with second ball of dough.

5 When pasta is dry, bring a large pot of salted water to the boil with 1 tablespoon vegetable oil. When the water is at a rolling boil, add the noodles all at once and stir. Allow the water to come to a second boil and begin testing for doneness.

When noodles are tender, drain well and place in a serving bowl.

6 Cut butter into slivers and toss with noodles. Spoon sour cream into center of noodles. Sprinkle orange rind, nutmeg, and white pepper on top of sour cream. Cut remaining beets into cubes or small julienne pieces. Scatter around the edge of the noodles. Bring to the table and toss.

SPINACH AND PARSLEY SALAD WITH HOT ANCHOVY DRESSING

INGREDIENTS

*1½ cups spinach leaves,
   washed, dried and torn
   into bite-size pieces
½ cup Italian flat-leaf
   parsley, washed and patted
   dry
¼ cup olive oil
1 clove garlic, minced
½ teaspoon anchovy paste
2 teaspoons lemon juice
Salt and freshly ground black
   pepper to taste*

1 Combine spinach and parsley in a serving bowl.

2 In a small saucepan, heat oil over low heat. Add garlic and cook 2 to 3 minutes, until tender, not browned. Stir in anchovy paste and lemon juice. Season with salt and pepper. Immediately pour over salad greens. Toss well and serve while dressing is still warm.

NOTE *The combination of olive oil, garlic, anchovy paste, lemon juice, salt, and pepper makes a dynamic sauce for a quick spaghetti dish.*

In the top of a double boiler set over simmering water, combine 6 tablespoons unsalted butter, 2 tablespoons olive oil, and 3 to 4 minced cloves of garlic. Let the butter melt, stirring occasionally. Add 1 tablespoon anchovy paste and stir in. Add a generous dash of lemon juice and freshly ground black pepper to taste. Serve hot over 8 ounces of hot, cooked spaghetti.

OPPOSITE: Avocado, Orange, and Pecan Salad
(page 47).

PROSCIUTTO, PIMIENTO, AND CHEESE STRATA

INGREDIENTS

1 bay leaf
1 cup milk
4 slices Vienna bread, cut
  about ½ inch thick
1 jar (2 ounces) chopped
  pimientos, well drained
2 ounces sliced prosciutto
4 slices (4 ounces) Swiss
  cheese

1 tablespoon prepared
  mustard
2 eggs
Salt and freshly ground white
  pepper to taste

1 Preheat oven to 350 degrees.

2 Heat together bay leaf and milk. Simmer for 5 minutes, then remove from heat and allow to cool.

3 Grease a 1-quart casserole. Fit 2 bread slices (if necessary, cut bread to fit) in the bottom of the dish. Sprinkle pimientos over the bread. Tear or slice prosciutto into bite-size pieces and sprinkle over the pimiento. Cover with 2 cheese slices. Spread ½ tablespoon mustard over the cheese. Fit remaining bread over the cheese. Tear or cut remaining 2 cheese slices and sprinkle over the bread.

4 Remove the bay leaf from the milk and set on top of the cheese. Whisk together the milk, remaining ½ tablespoon mustard, eggs, salt, and white pepper. Pour into the dish.

5 Bake for 35 to 45 minutes, until the mixture is puffed and lightly browned. Remove from oven and set aside 5 minutes to cool. Cut in wedges.

NOTE *Recipe can be halved. Cut baking time to 20 to 30 minutes.*

OPPOSITE: Lamb Kabobs (page 79) with Bulgur Pilaf (page 80).

FRUITED BUTTERNUT SQUASH

INGREDIENTS

1 pound butternut squash
¼ cup coarsely chopped
  apricots
½ cup orange juice
2 tablespoons maple syrup
¼ teaspoon ground
  cinnamon
1 tablespoon butter

1 Preheat oven to 350 degrees.

2 Place squash upright on cookie sheet and bake for 45 minutes to 1 hour, or until knife tip can easily penetrate the squash.

3 Meanwhile, combine apricots and orange juice in small pot. Cook over low heat until orange juice is reduced to a thick syrup, measuring about 1 tablespoon. This takes about 15 to 20 minutes. Stir in maple syrup, cinnamon, and butter and cook over low heat just until butter melts. Set aside, covered.

4 When squash is tender, remove from oven and cut in half lengthwise. Remove and discard seeds. Spoon half of apricot mixture into each cavity. Serve hot.

NOTE *For a single-serving idea, substitute a sweet potato for the butternut squash.*
Pierce the potato several times with fork tines and bake in a preheated 375-degree oven for 45 minutes or until tender. Remove the potato; peel and slice ½ inch thick. Arrange the slices on a plate. Prepare the apricot mixture—it isn't necessary to reduce the amounts—and spoon over the sweet potato slices.

KIM UPTON'S SPICY SIRLOIN WITH BROWN RICE

INGREDIENTS

8 ounces boneless sirloin
2 tablespoons soy sauce
2 tablespoons red-wine vinegar
1 teaspoon sesame oil
1 teaspoon cornstarch
2 tablespoons water
2 tablespoons peanut oil
1 small onion, sliced
1 tablespoon minced gingerroot

2 green chilies, halved, but not seeded
2 carrots, diagonally sliced
1 can (3½ ounces) bamboo shoots, drained and julienned
1 tablespoon fresh coriander leaves (cilantro)
Cooked brown rice

1 Cut sirloin across the grain in slices ¼ inch thick and 3 inches wide.

2 In a small bowl, combine soy sauce, red-wine vinegar, sesame oil, cornstarch, and water. Stir to combine and set aside.

3 Heat 1 tablespoon peanut oil in a wok or large skillet. Add sirloin and cook, stirring constantly until outside of beef is brown, but inside is still red. Remove from wok and keep warm. Wipe out wok.

4 Heat remaining 1 tablespoon of the peanut oil in the wok or skillet. Add onion and cook, stirring constantly until onion is soft. Add gingerroot and chilies and cook 1 minute. Then add carrots and bamboo shoots and cook, stirring constantly, until carrots are tender, but not mushy. Return beef to wok. Stir sauce and pour into wok. Cook, stirring constantly, until sauce thickens. Remove chili halves and discard. Sprinkle meat with fresh coriander and serve with cooked brown rice.

KIM UPTON'S STRAW MUSHROOM SOUP

INGREDIENTS

1 can (about 14 ounces)
    chicken broth
1/4 cup dry Sherry
1/8 teaspoon freshly ground
    white pepper
1/3 cup canned straw
    mushrooms

1 teaspoon sesame oil
2 scallions, both white and
    green parts, sliced

1 In a small saucepan, combine chicken broth, Sherry, and white pepper.

2 Bring to a boil, reduce heat and add mushrooms and sesame oil. Heat for a minute. Just before serving, sprinkle with scallions.

NOTE *Canned straw mushrooms and sesame oil are available in oriental sections of supermarkets or oriental food stores.*

J A N U A R Y

CHAPTER

5

This is a soup and stew month; both dishes are culinary antifreeze.

Bean soup is a favorite cold-weather antidote. The soup, chock-full of carrots, bell peppers, tomatoes, and bacon, is a meal in a bowl. The recipe makes four servings; two for dinner and two for the freezer. Chewy, Herbed Breadsticks make a flavorful accompaniment.

It is possible to prepare a mouth-watering stew for two without getting silly about it (measuring fractions of carrots, for example), as the recipe for Beef Goulash proves. Serve the goulash over Spinach Spaetzle and enjoy.

As a note of explanation, both the soup and stew recipe use paprika; the Bean Soup uses hot paprika, which can be very spicy, and the Beef Goulash uses Hungarian sweet paprika. The package will indicate the type. With either kind, more flavor is released if the paprika is cooked in a little fat, rather than just sprinkled on a dish. Store paprika in the refrigerator for longer potency.

Arroz Con Pollo, a robust chicken, rice, and vegetable casserole, is festive enough for a special dinner for two. Serve it with a refreshing Avocado, Orange, and Pecan Salad. Use just enough honey in the lime mayonnaise-like dressing to avoid bitterness; any more would make the mixture cloyingly sweet.

To provide incentive to get out of bed on a blustery Sunday prepare a brunch menu featuring Egg and Broccoli Casserole and Scones. Save any leftover Scones from breakfast for afternoon tea. Slather whipped cream and jam on the scones and indulge.

BEAN SOUP

INGREDIENTS

1 cup navy beans
2 cups water
6 bacon slices
1 carrot, peeled and diced
1 red bell pepper, cored,
*   seeded, and diced*
1 small onion, peeled and
*   chopped*
1 large clove garlic, minced

½ teaspoon good-quality
*   medium-hot paprika*
3 cups chicken broth
1 can (1 pound) crushed
*   tomatoes*
1 bay leaf
Salt and freshly ground black
*   pepper to taste*

1   Place beans and water in a pot. Bring to a boil, cover and boil 1 minute. Remove from heat. Let beans stand, covered in the hot water for 1 hour. (This is the rapid method for soaking dried beans; the alternative is to cover the beans with water and set out on the counter overnight.)

2   Meanwhile, sauté bacon slices in a large pot until browned and crisp. Remove bacon and reserve.

3   Pour off all but 2 tablespoons fat. Add carrot and pepper and sauté 5 minutes. Add onion and garlic and sauté 5 more minutes. Then stir in paprika. Allow mixture to brown slightly. Stir constantly for 2 minutes. Add a little of the chicken broth and stir up browned bits on the bottom of the pot. Then add 2 cups chicken broth. Stir in crushed tomatoes, bay leaf, salt, and pepper (if using canned chicken broth, taste the mixture in the Dutch oven before salting).

4   Drain water off beans and add beans to soup. Stir and bring to a boil. Reduce heat to low, cover, and simmer soup 2½ to 3 hours, or until beans are as tender as desired. Add remaining chicken broth to thin the soup. Remove bay leaf. Crumble bacon and sprinkle into each serving.

SERVES 4

HERBED BREADSTICKS

INGREDIENTS

½ cup milk
¼ cup very warm water
1¼ teaspoons active dry yeast
  (about ½ package)
1½ to 1¾ cups all-purpose
  flour
½ teaspoon salt
1 tablespoon dried, crushed
  oregano

1 tablespoon vegetable oil
2 tablespoons cornmeal
1 egg white, lightly beaten

1 Preheat oven to 400 degrees.

2 Heat milk to scalding, then cool until barely hot (warmer than lukewarm). Meanwhile, pour water into a small cup and sprinkle in yeast. Stir and let sit for 10 minutes until mixture becomes foamy.

3 Meanwhile, in large bowl combine 1 cup flour, salt, and oregano. Pour in yeast mixture, oil, and barely hot ½ cup milk. Stir well with a wooden spoon to form a moist batter. Stir in ¼ cup additional flour to make a sticky dough. Add more flour by the tablespoonful until dough can be turned out onto a floured board and kneaded.

4 Knead until smooth and elastic, adding as little additional flour as necessary. This should take about 10 minutes.

5 Sprinkle a cookie sheet with cornmeal.

6 Divide dough into 8 equal parts. Roll each into an 8-inch stick. Place on the cookie sheet, allowing at least an inch between breadsticks. Brush each stick with egg white.

7 Bake for 25 minutes. Cool for 5 minutes, then carefully remove from cookie sheet.

MAKES 8 BREADSTICKS

BEEF GOULASH

INGREDIENTS

1 tablespoon butter
1 tablespoon vegetable oil
1 medium onion, peeled and
  sliced
2 tablespoons all-purpose
  flour
Salt and freshly ground black
  pepper to taste
½ pound beef for stew, cut
  into cubes

1½ teaspoons good-quality
  Hungarian sweet paprika
2 cups beef broth
½ teaspoon crushed dill seed
½ cup sliced carrots
½ cup sour cream
Spinach Spaetzle (recipe
  follows)

1 Heat butter and oil together in a large pot. Separate onion slices into rings and cook in butter-oil mixture over moderate heat until transparent, about 5 minutes. Remove and set aside.

2 Combine flour with salt and pepper. Coat meat with flour mixture, shaking off excess. Brown half the meat at a time in the remaining fat. Remove meat to brown the second half. Stir in paprika. Stir constantly with a wooden spoon and allow paprika to brown slightly and become fragrant.

3 Stir in ½ cup beef broth and scrape up bits from the bottom of the pot. Add remaining beef broth, browned beef, onion rings, and dill seed. Cover and simmer over low heat 1½ hours. Stir in carrots and cook 15 minutes more or until carrots are tender. Place sour cream in a small bowl. Stir some of the hot beef liquid into the sour cream to warm it up. Then gently stir cream into the beef goulash. Do not allow the goulash to boil at this point or the sour cream will curdle. Serve hot over Spinach Spaetzle.

SPINACH SPAETZLE

INGREDIENTS

*1 firmly packed cup washed
  and dried spinach leaves*
¾ cup all-purpose flour
Pinch of ground nutmeg
¼ teaspoon salt
1 egg, beaten
3 to 5 tablespoons milk

1½ tablespoons butter
*Salt and freshly ground white
  pepper to taste*

1 Steam spinach leaves 3 to 5 minutes. Drain, then squeeze dry. Mince.

2 Sift together flour, nutmeg, and salt. Beat in spinach and egg. Add milk by the tablespoon to get a consistency that is very thick and sticky, but not as dry as dough.

3 Bring a large pot of water to a rolling boil. Place the spinach mixture on a wet dinner plate. Dip a knife in the boiling water. Holding the plate over the water, cut off slivers of dough and drop in the water. Wet knife occasionally. Stir occasionally so spaetzle don't stick to the bottom of the pot. When spaetzle float to the surface of the water, test for doneness. Spaetzle should be chewy, not gummy. Drain well and set aside.

4 Melt butter in a large skillet. Add all the spaetzle at once and sauté over low heat until coated with butter and hot. Season with salt and white pepper.

ARROZ CON POLLO

INGREDIENTS

3 tablespoons vegetable oil
4 chicken thigh pieces (or a
  combination of thighs and
  drumsticks)
1 small onion, peeled and
  chopped
1 clove garlic, minced
1/2 cup rice
1/8 teaspoon crushed saffron
  soaked in 1 or 2 teaspoons
  warm water for 5 minutes

1/2 teaspoon salt
1/8 teaspoon crushed red
  pepper flakes
1/4 teaspoon freshly ground
  black pepper
1 cup hot chicken broth
2 tablespoons chopped
  pimiento
1 cup fresh or frozen, thawed
  peas

1 Heat oil in large, heavy-bottomed skillet. Add chicken pieces and brown on both sides over medium heat, about 10 minutes total. Remove from skillet and keep warm.

2 Pour off all but 2 tablespoons fat. Add onion and garlic to skillet and sauté over medium heat about 5 minutes, until onions are transparent. Add rice and stir briefly until grains are glossy.

3 Meanwhile, stir saffron with water, salt, red pepper flakes, and pepper into hot broth until saffron dissolves.

4 Pour broth mixture into rice mixture. Bring to a boil. Reduce heat to low and stir. Add chicken, cover, and simmer about 20 minutes, stirring occasionally, or until rice is tender and liquid is absorbed (using a heavy-bottomed skillet and very low heat is the key to preventing the rice from sticking, although it will take longer than usual to cook).

5 Stir in the pimiento and peas. Cook over low heat about 5 minutes, stirring occasionally until peas are heated through. Serve immediately.

PHOTO OPPOSITE PAGE 21. SERVES 2 GENEROUSLY

AVOCADO, ORANGE, AND PECAN SALAD

INGREDIENTS

*1 small navel orange, peeled
 and sectioned
1 medium avocado, peeled
 and sliced
1 egg, at room temperature
1 tablespoon lime juice
1 tablespoon grated lime rind
Dash of salt
½ to 1 tablespoon honey*

*½ cup vegetable oil
2 tablespoons chopped
 pecans*

1 Arrange orange and avocado sections alternatively in circle on serving plate.

2 In a blender or food processor, combine egg, lime juice, lime rind, salt, and honey. Process 30 seconds, until smooth. With machine running, slowly trickle in oil to make a thick, smooth, mayonnaise-like mixture.

3 Spoon about ¼ cup of the lime dressing over the orange and avocado sections making a ring around the center. Sprinkle on pecans. Serve immediately.

PHOTO OPPOSITE PAGE 36

NOTE *To make this salad for one, use half an orange and half an avocado. Also use only 1 tablespoon chopped pecans.*

   The recipe makes about ¾ cup dressing and it is difficult to reduce. However, the remainder can be stored, covered, in the refrigerator for 2 days. It makes a wonderful alternative to plain mayonnaise in a fruit salad, chicken salad, or Waldorf salad.

EGG AND BROCCOLI CASSEROLE

INGREDIENTS

1 cup broccoli flowerets
1 tablespoon butter
1 tablespoon all-purpose flour
½ cup milk, heated
½ cup grated Cheddar cheese
Dash of cayenne pepper
Salt and freshly ground white
*   pepper to taste*
2 eggs

1 Preheat oven to 400 degrees.

2 Cut broccoli into small pieces, about 1 inch each. Bring a medium pot filled with water to a boil. Add broccoli and cook 5 to 8 minutes. Remove broccoli and set aside to drain thoroughly.

3 Melt butter in a small saucepan. Add flour and stir well to make a frothy mixture. Gradually add milk, stirring constantly to make a thick mixture. Stir in cheese, mixing until cheese completely melts in. Stir in seasonings and remove cheese mixture from heat.

4 Fit broccoli into bottom of 2-cup oven-proof casserole, making an even layer. Cover with cheese sauce. Break eggs over top. Cover loosely with greased foil. Bake for 20 to 30 minutes, or until eggs are cooked to desired doneness. Remove foil. Serve immediately.

SERVES 1

SCONES

INGREDIENTS

1 cup all-purpose flour
¼ teaspoon salt
1 teaspoon sugar
1 teaspoon baking powder
2 tablespoons unsalted butter
5 to 7 tablespoons heavy
*   cream*
1 to 2 tablespoons milk

1 Preheat oven to 425 degrees.

2 Sift together flour, salt, sugar, and baking powder 10 times. Cut butter in small pieces and cut into flour mixture. Pour in cream by the tablespoonful to create a dough that will hold together. Knead 3 or 4 times.

3 On a floured surface, pat dough into a rectangle. Roll ½ inch thick. Cut into 2-inch rounds. Place 2 inches apart on a greased cookie sheet. Brush the top of each scone with milk. Bake for 13 to 15 minutes, or until the scones are lightly browned. Serve warm or cold.

MAKES 6 SCONES

NOTE *There are as many ways to make scones as there are scone lovers.*
    Many British recipes omit sugar and use baking soda and cream of tartar as leavening agents. Buttermilk or soured milk is a key part of this combination. Most American recipes use sugar, and call for either baking powder or baking soda and cream of tartar to give the biscuit its characteristic lightness.
    Americans butter their scones, while the British slather them with cream.
    The above recipe takes the best qualities of all scones. The secret to this version is to sift the dry ingredients together 10 times. (That's the difference between a scone and a stone.) Once the dough is mixed, don't overhandle it or the scones will be tough. Serve within a few hours of baking or freeze.

FEBRUARY

CHAPTER

6

A craving for high-carbohydrate foods seems natural during the winter. Pasta, rice, and potatoes are energy and heat boosters that help keep you warm.

One rich, delicious, and fattening (you can't avoid all calories in life) way to enjoy carbohydrates is in a dish of Tortellini in Blue Cheese Sauce. Tortellini is available fresh, frozen, or dried, using spinach or plain pasta and with cheese, spinach, or meat filling. The meat filling is too heavy for this dish, but any of the other choices will work. Serve the tortellini with a quick version of Caesar Salad, which has all the flavor and none of the fuss of the real thing.

Although risotto, the Italian rice dish, requires constant attention the results are well worth it. The texture is creamy, yet chewy; the flavor well developed, yet not overwhelming. A meal of Chicken Livers Risotto with an Avocado and Sesame Salad is the next best thing to a fur coat to keep the chill away.

Make Valentine's Day a spicy celebration with garlicky, gingery Barbecued Drumsticks. Round out the meal with a pungent Pea Salad and almost tame Thai Carrots. It's the start of a hot night. Or serve Garlicky Shrimp with Whole-Wheat French Bread for messy, butter-dripping, finger-licking food that's wonderful.

Apples and pork are natural companions. Pan-Simmered Pork Chops pairs these ingredients to maximum advantage. Roast Potato with Garlic and Rosemary completes the entree.

TORTELLINI IN BLUE CHEESE SAUCE

INGREDIENTS

6 cups water
1 tablespoon vegetable oil
Salt
¼ pound cheese- or
  spinach-filled fresh or
  frozen tortellini
½ cup heavy cream
1½ ounces Gorgonzola
  cheese

1 tablespoon butter
Freshly ground black pepper
  to taste

1 Heat water to boiling in a medium pot. Add oil and a dash of salt. Pour in tortellini and allow water to come to a second boil. Reduce heat to medium. Cooking time will vary according to the product. When tortellini float to the surface, start testing.

2 In the meantime, in a heavy-bottomed skillet, heat the cream to boiling over medium heat. Boil until cream is reduced by a third. Crumble in cheese and mash into the cream until the mixture becomes thick and smooth. Remove from heat. Cut butter into slivers and whisk into cream.

3 Drain tortellini well. Add to cream mixture and toss well. If necessary, reheat briefly over low heat. Season well with pepper. Serve immediately.

SERVES 1 TO 2

OPPOSITE: Chicken with Orange and Brandy
(page 90), served with Fragrant Brown Rice
(page 91).

CAESAR SALAD

INGREDIENTS

¹/₄ teaspoon minced garlic
(1 small clove)
1 egg yolk
¹/₄ teaspoon Worcestershire
sauce
1¹/₂ teaspoons anchovy paste
1¹/₂ teaspoons freshly grated
Parmesan cheese
1¹/₂ teaspoons white wine
vinegar

2¹/₂ tablespoons olive oil
Freshly ground black pepper
to taste
3 cups torn romaine lettuce
¹/₂ cup croutons

1 In blender, food processor, or by hand, combine garlic, egg yolk, Worcestershire, anchovy paste, Parmesan, vinegar, and oil. Season with black pepper.

2 Place lettuce and croutons in a bowl. Pour on all or part of dressing, according to personal preference. Toss well and serve immediately.

MAKES ABOUT ¼ CUP DRESSING

NOTE *Because the dressing for this salad uses a raw egg, it is essential that the egg be fresh and that the dressing and salad be prepared just before serving.*
If you wish, you can make the dressing in advance, omitting the egg. The dressing can be stored in the refrigerator several days. Bring to room temperature and add the egg.
To make croutons, cut a ¹/₂-inch-thick slice of French bread. Heat together 2 tablespoons vegetable or olive oil and 1 crushed clove of garlic. Pour the oil over the bread to cover it; all the oil may not be used. Then toast the bread in a preheated 400-degree oven for 5 to 10 minutes, until lightly browned. Break or cut the bread into pieces.

OPPOSITE: Fish Stew (page 94).

CHICKEN LIVERS RISOTTO

INGREDIENTS

2 to 3 tablespoons butter
¼ pound mushrooms,
cleaned and sliced
½ pound chicken livers, with
lobes separated
3 tablespoons clarified butter
1 medium onion, peeled and
chopped
¾ cup Italian arborio rice (see note)

¼ cup Soave or other dry
white wine
3 cups good-quality chicken
broth
⅛ teaspoon crushed saffron
¼ cup freshly grated
Parmesan cheese
Salt and freshly ground white
pepper to taste

1 Melt 2 tablespoons butter in a large skillet. Add mushrooms and sauté until lightly browned, about 5 minutes. Remove. If necessary, add another tablespoon butter and cook chicken livers over medium heat, until browned on the outside, but still pink inside, about 3 to 5 minutes. Remove and set aside with the mushrooms. Wipe out the skillet.

2 Heat 3 tablespoons clarified butter in the skillet. Add onion and sauté until transparent, about 5 minutes. Add rice and cook over low heat, stirring until the grains are glossy and slightly transparent, about 5 minutes. Stir in wine and allow to evaporate. Meanwhile heat broth and keep over low heat.

3 Add about ⅓ cup broth to the rice, stirring occasionally. Allow the broth to be absorbed. The rice should neither cook too fast nor too slow. The broth should take 4 or 5 minutes to be absorbed. Each time the broth is absorbed, add another ⅓ cup and stir occasionally. When half the broth is finished, set aside ⅓ cup and dissolve the saffron in it. Add the saffron mixture to the rice (saffron added halfway through the cooking will give a nice, not too assertive flavor). Continue adding broth and stirring occasionally until rice is tender, with the slightest firmness in the center and the mixture a creamy consistency. This takes 30 to 40 minutes.

4 Drain off any juices from the mushrooms and livers. Stir in both and heat through. Sprinkle on cheese and stir. Taste and season with salt and white pepper. Serve immediately.

NOTE *Small, fat-grained arborio rice is available in gourmet or Italian food stores. Regular long-grain rice can substitute, but the consistency of the finished dish won't be as creamy.*

AVOCADO AND SESAME SALAD

INGREDIENTS

½ medium avocado, peeled and sliced
1 scallion, green part only, sliced
2 cups torn lettuce (Bibb or Boston)
4 teaspoons soy sauce
4 teaspoons vegetable oil
½ teaspoon toasted sesame seeds (see note)

½ teaspoon prepared mustard
1½ teaspoons red-wine vinegar
Pinch of sugar
Salt and freshly ground black pepper to taste

1 Combine avocado, scallion, and lettuce in a salad bowl.

2 Whisk together soy sauce, oil, sesame seeds, mustard, vinegar, sugar, salt, and pepper. Pour over avocado mixture. Serve immediately.

NOTE *To toast sesame seeds, place in a small, dry skillet over medium heat and cook a few minutes, stirring or shaking the skillet constantly until seeds are lightly browned. Watch carefully.*

To give this salad a special look, arrange lettuce leaves on 2 salad plates—a total of 6 Bibb or Boston leaves should do. Then arrange avocado slices in pinwheel shapes on top of the lettuce. Dice the scallions and sprinkle over the avocado. Prepare the dressing and pour over the salads. Garnish the center of each salad with a cherry tomato for contrasting color.

BARBECUED DRUMSTICKS

INGREDIENTS

1 tablespoon vegetable oil
1 large clove garlic, minced
1 tablespoon minced
*   gingerroot*
3 tablespoons honey
3 tablespoons lemon juice
1 tablespoon tomato paste

Salt and freshly ground black
*   pepper to taste*
4 chicken drumsticks

1 Heat oil in a medium pot. Sauté garlic and gingerroot over low heat for 5 minutes. Add honey, lemon juice, tomato paste, salt, and pepper. Simmer 5 minutes. Remove from heat.

2 Add drumsticks and let marinate for 30 minutes, turning occasionally.

3 Preheat oven to 400 degrees.

4 Place chicken on a cooling rack set over a foil-lined jelly-roll pan. Cook chicken for 30 to 35 minutes, basting with any remaining marinade every 15 minutes. Turn drumsticks over halfway through cooking time. Drumsticks will brown nicely. If a darker and crisper skin is desired, turn on broiler and broil drumsticks for 1 to 3 minutes. Watch closely to avoid burning.

NOTE *For parties, substitute chicken wings for a managable hors d'oeuvre. Cut each wing into 2 portions and follow the recipe, cutting the cooking time to 15 to 20 minutes. This recipe makes enough marinade for 8 chicken wings.*
*   To make the drumstick recipe for one, prepare the same amount of marinade, but use only 2 drumsticks.*

PEA SALAD

INGREDIENTS

1 cup frozen peas, thawed
½ cup sour cream or plain
   yogurt
¼ teaspoon freshly ground
   white pepper
¼ teaspoon salt
1 tablespoon chopped chives
   or grated onion
1 rounded tablespoon minced
   pimiento

1 Taste one pea and if it isn't tender (some brands need further cooking, others don't) bring 1 cup of water to the boil in a small pot. Add the peas and cook for 5 minutes. Drain and cool completely.

2 Place peas in a serving bowl. Spoon in sour cream or yogurt, chives or onion, and pimiento. Stir gently, but well. Some of the red from the pimiento will fade into the sour cream, but this is a desirable effect. Chill the salad for at least 1 hour before serving.

NOTE *Don't make this recipe more than 24 hours in advance or the colors will become too muddy.*
   Recipe can be halved.

THAI CARROTS

INGREDIENTS

4 small carrots, pared and
   shredded
1 teaspoon sugar
1 teaspoon lemon juice
1 small clove garlic, minced
2 teaspoons nam pla *(see*
   note)
⅛ teaspoon chili oil

1 Place carrots in a salad bowl. Combine sugar and lemon juice and stir to dissolve sugar. Add garlic, *nam pla*, and chili oil.

2 Pour sauce over carrots, toss well, and set aside for 30 minutes for flavors to blend.

NOTE *The dressing for the carrots can also be used for sliced cucumbers. Simply substitute 2 large, thinly sliced cucumbers for the carrots.*
   Nam Pla is a fish-based sauce that is as important in Thai cuisine as soy sauce is in Chinese cooking. It has a flavor that is salty and sharp, but not especially fishy. It is available in Thai, Philippine, and some Chinese grocery stores. It is unique, but 1 teaspoon light soy sauce plus 1 teaspoon vegetable oil could be substituted in the carrot recipe.

GARLICKY SHRIMP

INGREDIENTS

½ cup butter
¼ cup vegetable oil
2 cloves garlic, minced
2 bay leaves
½ teaspoon crushed, dried
  oregano
Salt and freshly ground black
  pepper to taste

1 teaspoon crushed red
  pepper flakes
Dash of lemon juice
1 pound medium to large
  shrimp in the shell

1 Melt the butter in a 3-quart pot or skillet with a lid. Remove from heat. Add oil, garlic, bay leaves, oregano, salt, pepper, red pepper flakes, lemon juice, and shrimp. Toss well. Set aside for 30 minutes (butter may solidify), stirring occasionally.

2 Place the pot over low to medium heat and allow to come to a bubble gently, not vigorously. Stir. Cover and cook shrimp 5 minutes or just until they turn bright pink.

3 Spoon shrimp into 2 serving bowls. Divide pan juices between the servings. Serve immediately.

NOTE *The shrimp can be peeled first, but they will have more flavor if cooked in the shell.*

WHOLE-WHEAT FRENCH BREAD

INGREDIENTS

1 package active dry yeast
1 teaspoon sugar
1 cup very warm water
2 tablespoons olive oil
1 teaspoon salt
1¼ cups all-purpose flour
1 cup whole-wheat flour
Cornmeal

1 Combine yeast, sugar, and ¼ cup warm water in a cup. Stir and set aside for 5 minutes for yeast to foam. Add olive oil, stirring in.

2 Stir together salt, 1 cup all-purpose flour, and 1 cup whole-wheat flour in a large bowl. Pour in the yeast mixture and remaining ¾ cup warm water. Mix well with a wooden spoon.

3 Turn out dough onto a floured board using the remaining ¼ cup all-purpose flour, and knead 10 minutes. Place dough in a greased bowl, turning to grease all sides. Cover with a cloth towel. Place the bowl in a warm area to rise 1 hour.

4 Punch dough down and divide in half. Shape each half into a long loaf. Place loaves on a pan dusted with cornmeal. Make 1 or 2 diagonal slashes in top of each loaf. Cover with a towel and allow to rise again for 30 minutes.

5 Preheat the oven to 375 degrees. Bake breads for 30 minutes, or until they are golden and done. Remove from the oven and cool. Serve slightly warm or cold.

NOTE *Although it is a nice gesture to serve one bread per person, it is unlikely that an individual can eat an entire loaf. As soon as the breads are cold, you can wrap one in foil and freeze it for another meal.*

PAN-SIMMERED PORK CHOPS

INGREDIENTS

*¾ teaspoon good-quality hot
  paprika, divided*
*2 tablespoons all-purpose
  flour*
*Salt and freshly ground black
  pepper to taste*
*2 pork chops (total of ¾
  pound), each ¾ inch thick*
*2 tablespoons vegetable
  shortening*

1 can (5 ounces) apple juice
Pinch of sugar
*Dash of balsamic or cider
  vinegar*

1 Combine ½ teaspoon paprika, flour, salt, and pepper to taste on a plate. Dust pork chops on both sides in flour mixture.

2 Heat shortening in skillet. Add pork and brown on both sides, allowing about 8 minutes per side. Remove from skillet and keep warm. Pour off all but a film of fat. Add remaining ¼ teaspoon paprika to the skillet and cook over low heat 1 minute.

3 Add apple juice and cook over high heat 3 to 5 minutes, stirring up browned bits on bottom of the skillet, until liquid thickens and is reduced by a fourth. Add sugar and vinegar. Season with salt and pepper. Return pork to skillet. Partially cover and simmer 5 minutes to flavor pork. Serve with pan juices.

ROAST POTATO WITH GARLIC AND ROSEMARY

INGREDIENTS

2 tablespoons butter, divided
1½ tablespoons olive oil
1 large potato
2 large cloves garlic, peeled
  and sliced paper thin
Salt and freshly ground black
  pepper to taste
About 6 sprigs (1 inch each)
  fresh rosemary or ½
  teaspoon dried rosemary

1 Preheat oven to 325 degrees.

2 In a small skillet, heat together 1½ tablespoons butter and the oil. Pour a small amount into the bottom of a 2-cup oven-proof casserole.

3 Slice potato ⅛ inch thick (it doesn't have to be peeled). Place a layer of potato slices over butter mixture. Top with a garlic layer. Sprinkle with a little salt and pepper. Pour on a little more butter mixture. Repeat layering twice more, ending with a light sprinkling of salt and pepper. Tuck rosemary sprigs into the casserole. If using dried rosemary instead, sprinkle on at the same time salt and pepper are being layered in. Dot the top of the dish with the remaining ½ tablespoon butter.

4 Bake for 45 minutes, basting every 15 minutes with butter mixture from the bottom of the dish. When potatoes are tender, either remove from the oven and serve, or turn the heat up to 550 degrees and bake 5 minutes to brown.

MARCH

CHAPTER

7 Cooking during March has its frustrations. The offerings in the supermarket seem as predictable and tired as those in the clothes closet after a long winter's wear. This then is a month for highly flavored foods to make meals more appealing.

To start, there's a deceptively simple entree of Scallops with Angel-Hair Pasta. It's slightly biting, slightly innocent, and very satisfying. A wholesome Spinach-Mushroom Salad is a nice accent for the pasta.

Greek-Style Beef Stew calls for cinnamon and nutmeg in a spicy-sweet blend. Inexpensive stew meat is the best choice for this slow-cooking dish. While you wait for the stew, appease hunger pangs with Eggplant Spread, a Middle Eastern dish of cumin, eggplant, and tahini. The spread is excellent with toasted pita bread quarters or fresh vegetables.

The pot pie, admittedly old-fashioned, is returning to favor. It's economical, makes good use of leftovers, is easy to prepare, and tastes good. Chicken Pot Pie, brimming with chicken and vegetables and topped with baking-powder biscuits, showcases this dish at its best. Serve it alone or with a peppery Watercress Salad.

Finally, just before shedding winter recipes, try Sauerbraten Meatballs with a vegetable course of Cumin Beans and Onions.

Winter wasn't so bad, was it?

SCALLOPS WITH ANGEL-HAIR PASTA

INGREDIENTS

½ pound bay scallops
1 large clove garlic, minced
6 tablespoons olive oil,
divided
¼ teaspoon crushed red
pepper flakes
8 ounces angel-hair or thin
spaghetti

Salt and freshly ground white
pepper to taste
1 tablespoon chopped parsley

1 Rinse scallops and pat dry.

2 Sauté garlic in 4 tablespoons olive oil in a medium skillet for 5 minutes over low heat. Don't let the garlic burn. Add red pepper flakes and cook a few seconds. Add scallops. Turn up heat to medium high and cook scallops for 1 minute, stirring constantly until scallops turn opaque. Do not overcook. Remove from heat and set aside.

3 Add angel-hair spaghetti to a large pot of boiling water combined with 1 tablespoon olive oil. Stir gently to separate strands and bring to a second boil. Reduce heat to medium and cook at a low boil until pasta is tender (this can take from 3 to 8 minutes, depending on brand and thinness of spaghetti).

4 Drain immediately and stir into skillet with scallops. Turn heat to low and toss mixture to coat with oil and seasonings. Add remaining tablespoon oil to make pasta glisten and adjust red pepper flakes to taste.

5 This dish should have a little bite, but not be overwhelming. Season with salt and white pepper. Garnish with parsley and toss gently. Serve immediately.

SPINACH-MUSHROOM SALAD

INGREDIENTS

*1½ cups spinach leaves
    (measured after washing,
    stemming and tearing into
    pieces; purchase about 5
    ounces)*
½ cup sliced mushrooms
1 egg
*1 teaspoon prepared white
    horseradish*

Dash salt
*Freshly ground white pepper
    to taste*
*1 tablespoon white wine
    vinegar*
¼ cup vegetable oil
2 teaspoons poppy seeds

1 Place spinach and mushrooms in salad bowl and set aside.

2 In the bowl of a food processor fitted with a steel blade or blender, place egg, horseradish, salt, white pepper, and vinegar. Whirl about 10 seconds to combine. With machine running, dribble in oil as for mayonnaise. Then with machine off, stir in poppy seeds.

3 This dressing will be frothy, but not thick like a mayonnaise. Spoon half over the salad. Remaining half can be kept covered in the refrigerator up to 2 days. Whisk well before using.

MAKES ABOUT ⅔ CUP DRESSING

GREEK-STYLE BEEF STEW

INGREDIENTS

½ cup vegetable oil
1 large onion, peeled and
  sliced
½ cup all-purpose flour
2 pounds beef stew meat, cut
  in cubes
2 cloves garlic, peeled and
  crushed
½ cup dry red wine
1 can (1 pound) peeled
  tomatoes

2 bay leaves
½ teaspoon each ground
  cinnamon and nutmeg
¼ teaspoon ground cumin
1 can (8 ounces) tomato
  sauce
Salt and freshly ground black
  pepper to taste
Cooked noodles or rice

1 Heat oil in a large pot. Add the onion and sauté over low heat until transparent, about 5 minutes.

2 Meanwhile, pour flour into a bag. Add a few beef cubes and toss well. Push the onion slices to the side and add part of the beef cubes to brown on both sides over medium heat. Remove the beef cubes and continue browning the remainder. As you get to the last batch of beef, add the garlic but do not let it brown. Remove beef, garlic, and onions and set aside.

3 Pour off fat. Over low heat, add the red wine to the pot and stir to scrape up bits from the bottom. Return meat, garlic, and onions to the pot. Add the tomatoes, bay leaves, cinnamon, nutmeg, cumin, and tomato sauce. Stir well. Cover and simmer 2 hours. Before serving, taste and season with salt and pepper. Serve hot over noodles or rice.

SERVES 6

NOTE *Freeze leftovers in single-serving containers with ½ cup of cooked noodles or rice per container.*

EGGPLANT SPREAD

INGREDIENTS

1 small eggplant (about ¾ pound)
Salt
2 tablespoons olive oil
1 clove garlic, peeled
½ teaspoon cumin seeds
2 tablespoons fresh, minced Italian parsley
3 tablespoons fresh lemon juice

2 tablespoons tahini (see note)
Freshly ground white pepper to taste
2 pita breads, toasted

1 Preheat oven to 400 degrees.

2 Cut eggplant in half lengthwise. Salt both halves well and set aside for 30 minutes. Wipe off salt and accumulated liquids. Place eggplant halves on a cookie sheet. Brush each half with 1 tablespoon oil. Bake for 30 minutes, or until flesh is very tender. Cool and scoop out flesh. Discard skin.

3 In food processor fitted with steel blade or blender, puree eggplant flesh, garlic, cumin, and Italian parsley to get a thick, pulpy mixture. Remove to a bowl. Alternately add lemon juice and tahini to the mixture, stirring after each addition. Taste and season with salt and white pepper. Serve immediately or chill. Serve with hot toasted pita bread, cut into wedges.

NOTE *Tahini, a sesame-seed paste, is sold in Middle-Eastern sections of grocery stores.*

CHICKEN POT PIE

INGREDIENTS

2 chicken breast halves
1 can (about 14 ounces)
   chicken broth
2 tablespoons butter
$\frac{1}{2}$ cup finely diced carrots
$\frac{1}{4}$ cup finely diced celery
$\frac{1}{4}$ cup finely diced onion
2 tablespoons all-purpose
   flour

$\frac{1}{4}$ to $\frac{1}{2}$ teaspoon fresh,
   minced, or $\frac{1}{8}$ teaspoon
   crushed, dried thyme
Salt and freshly ground black
   pepper to taste
$\frac{1}{2}$ cup frozen or fresh peas
Drop Biscuits (recipe fol-
   lows)

1 Preheat oven to 350 degrees.

2 Place chicken breast halves in a medium pot with chicken broth. Cover and simmer about 30 minutes, or until chicken is done. Remove chicken and allow to cool, then remove the meat from the bones. Strain off 1 cup of chicken broth and set aside (remainder can be refrigerated or frozen for another use), keeping hot.

3 Melt butter in a medium pot. Add carrots and sauté over low heat for 5 minutes. Add celery and onion and sauté an additional 5 minutes. Stir in flour and cook to form a smooth paste. Gradually stir in the reserved 1 cup chicken broth, stirring constantly to form a smooth, thickened mixture. Stir in thyme, salt, and pepper. Then stir in peas and reserved chicken.

4 Spoon the chicken mixture into a 1-quart casserole. Set aside. Prepare Drop Biscuits. Drop by heaping tablespoonfuls onto the chicken mixture, forming 4 or 5 biscuits. Bake the pie for 30 minutes. Serve immediately.

OPPOSITE: Chicken Pot Pie.

DROP BISCUITS

INGREDIENTS

½ cup all-purpose flour
Dash each salt and sugar
1 teaspoon baking powder
2 tablespoons butter
5 tablespoons milk

1 Place flour, salt, sugar, and baking powder in a mixing bowl and stir.

2 Cut butter into thin slivers. Cut butter into dry ingredients, using 2 knives or a pastry blender, until the mixture resembles small peas.

3 Add the milk and toss briefly but well until a sticky dough is formed.

MAKES 4 OR 5 BISCUITS

OPPOSITE: Poached Eggs, Artichokes, and
Mayonnaise Sauce (page 81).

WATERCRESS SALAD

INGREDIENTS

1 teaspoon lemon juice
2 tablespoons olive oil
1 teaspoon prepared mustard
Salt to taste and a generous
   dash freshly ground black
   pepper
½ cup packed watercress
   leaves
1½ cups packed, torn Boston
   lettuce leaves

1 In a bowl, whisk together the lemon juice, oil, mustard, salt, and pepper.

2 Combine the watercress and lettuce in a salad bowl. Pour on the dressing and toss gently but well. Serve immediately.

NOTE *Watercress is one of the best, and most overlooked flavoring agents a head of lettuce could be matched with. It has a peppery taste that enlivens a salad.*

It used to be an exotic commodity but is now available almost the year round in supermarket produce counters. It is sold by the bunch. Since it is very delicate, either plan to use it the same day you buy it, or wrap the bunch in a damp paper towel, then in plastic wrap. It will keep this way for 3 or 4 days.

To use, pick off the leaves and carefully wash them, as they attract a lot of dirt. If you like, you can puree the leftover leaves and stems to include in a cream soup, such as the Watercress-Scallop Soup on page 172. Watercress is particularly good in a potato, zucchini, or spinach soup.

SAUERBRATEN MEATBALLS

INGREDIENTS

1 slice firm white bread
1/4 cup milk
1/2 pound ground chuck
2 to 3 teaspoons fresh,
    minced or 1 teaspoon
    dried, crushed thyme
1 egg, beaten
Salt and freshly ground black
    pepper to taste
4 tablespoons all-purpose
    flour
4 tablespoons butter, divided

1 clove garlic, minced
1 small onion, peeled and
    chopped
1 cup beef broth, heated
1 cup beer
1 bay leaf
1 tablespoon red wine vinegar
3 to 4 tablespoons gingersnap
    crumbs
Cooked rice or noodles
    (optional)

1 Soak bread in milk for 10 minutes. Crumble bread, draining off excess milk. Combine bread with beef, half of fresh or crushed thyme, egg, salt, and pepper. Mixture will be fairly wet. Shape into 8 meatballs, patties, or logs.

2 Place flour on a dinner plate. Dust meatballs with flour, coating on all sides. Set aside.

3 Melt 2 tablespoons butter in large skillet. Sauté garlic and onion for 5 minutes. Push aside to one part of the skillet and add remaining butter. Brown meatballs over medium heat, turning carefully (meatballs are soft). Remove meatballs, garlic, and onion and set aside. Pour off any remaining fat.

4 Pour beef broth into skillet, scraping up any browned bits. Add beer, remaining thyme, bay leaf, and vinegar. Bring to a boil. Reduce heat to simmer. Return meatballs, garlic, and onions to skillet. Cover and simmer 30 minutes, spooning gravy over meatballs occasionally.

5 Stir in 3 tablespoons gingersnap crumbs, and stir gravy. Taste and add remaining tablespoon if necessary for slightly sweet, spicy taste. Gingersnaps act as a thickener, so don't overdo it. Season with salt and pepper if necessary. Serve plain or over cooked rice or noodles.

CUMIN BEANS AND ONIONS

INGREDIENTS

8 ounces fresh green beans
1 small onion
4 tablespoons butter
1 teaspoon cumin seeds
½ teaspoon salt
¼ teaspoon freshly ground
*   black pepper*
Dash of lemon juice

1 Cut tips off green beans. Wash under cold water. Cut long beans in half. Steam over boiling water for 10 minutes.

2 Meanwhile, peel onion. Cut into slices about ¾ inch thick. Melt butter in a large skillet. Add cumin seeds and sauté over low heat for 2 to 3 minutes, stirring frequently. Add onion and sauté 10 minutes, until lightly browned. Add green beans and cook for another 3 minutes. Add salt, pepper, and lemon juice. Serve hot.

NOTE *Cumin, a staple seasoning in Mexican and Indian cooking, is finally being discovered in this country. It resembles the caraway seed, but has a distinctive flavor that's slightly smoky and pungent.*

When the seeds are gently cooked, as they are in the Cumin Beans and Onions recipe, the full taste is released.

To transform this dish into a quick entree, add chicken to the recipe.

Sauté the onion slices in butter, adding a cup of raw chicken cubes to the skillet. Stir frequently so chicken is cooked throughout. If you like, add a cup of cherry tomatoes to the sauté as well. Increase the butter to a total of 6 tablespoons. The recipe can be halved.

APRIL

CHAPTER

8

Signs of spring are surely evident this month. Seasonal treats such as rhubarb, asparagus, artichokes, and strawberries should be in good supply throughout the country.

Smelt, another seasonal specialty, is most plentiful this month. It's usually pan or deep-fried, and eaten bones and all. This recipe for smelt is served with the Chestnut Street Grill's Tartar Sauce, a Chicago favorite. For a salad course prepare Sweet-Soy Slaw.

Greening the spring menu is a delight when you serve Avocado Soufflé as an appetizer course. The dish is surprisingly rich, yet light. Turkey Marsala, an inexpensive variation on veal marsala, is the entree.

Although lamb is in good supply the year round, it is still considered a spring specialty. Season ground lamb with plenty of fresh coriander, gingerroot, and cumin and form into Lamb Kabobs to broil or grill. Bulgur Pilaf has a nutty, sweet flavor that goes well with the lamb.

Turn artichokes into a floral bouquet for a brunch or lunch for two. Cook artichokes and arrange the leaves in concentric circles on a plate. A poached egg becomes the center and a mayonnaise sauce turns the leaves to ivory. For a more substantial meal, start with Watercress-Scallop Soup (page 172).

SMELT WITH THE CHESTNUT STREET GRILL'S TARTAR SAUCE

INGREDIENTS

Tartar Sauce (recipe follows)
½ to ¾ pound smelt or perch
  fillets
Oil for deep-fat frying
½ cup milk
1 egg
6 tablespoons all-purpose
  flour
¼ cup cornmeal

½ teaspoon baking powder
¼ teaspoon salt
Freshly ground white pepper
  to taste

1 Prepare Tartar Sauce and chill while preparing fish.

2 If using smelt, rinse under cold water and pat dry. If using perch, cut into diagonal strips, each about 3 inches long. Pat dry.

3 Heat 1 inch of oil to 375 degrees in a heavy-bottomed skillet.

4 Whisk together the milk and egg. Stir together the flour, cornmeal, baking powder, salt and white pepper. Whisk in the milk mixture until no lumps remain.

5 Dip the fish fingers or smelt into the batter, a few at a time. Then ease into hot oil, cooking 2 to 3 minutes per side, or until golden brown. Remove and drain on paper-towel lined plate. Serve immediately with Tartar Sauce.

TARTAR SAUCE

INGREDIENTS

*1 small new potato (about ⅓
  cup)
1 cup mayonnaise
2 teaspoons minced red onion
½ teaspoon drained pickle
  relish
½ teaspoon minced fresh
  parsley*

1   Peel potato. Cube and place in a small pot of boiling water. Reduce heat. Simmer until potato pieces are so well done they begin to fall apart, about 20 to 30 minutes. Strain off all water and dry potato pieces. Cool 10 minutes. While still warm, mash to a pulp. Do not use a blender or food processor or potatoes will become pasty.

2   Add mayonnaise, red onion, pickle relish, and parsley and whisk for 5 minutes until sauce becomes light and creamy.

MAKES ABOUT 1 CUP

SWEET-SOY SLAW

INGREDIENTS

1½ tablespoons sugar
2 tablespoons dark soy sauce
1½ tablespoons cider vinegar
2 tablespoons vegetable oil
2 cups firmly packed coarsely
  shredded cabbage
1 cup coarsely shredded
  carrots
Freshly ground black pepper
  to taste

1 In a small pot, combine the sugar, soy sauce, and cider vinegar. Bring to a boil, stirring to dissolve sugar. Remove from heat. Stir in the oil.

2 In a salad bowl, toss together the cabbage and carrots. Pour half the warm dressing over the vegetables and toss well. The heat of the salad dressing will wilt the salad slightly. Add more dressing as desired. I prefer this salad well flavored. Season with a generous amount of pepper.

3 If the salad is served immediately it will retain much of its crunch. However, if you like, let it sit at room temperature for 30 minutes before serving, and the vegetables will become very tender. Serve either way.

AVOCADO SOUFFLÉ

INGREDIENTS

2 tablespoons unsalted butter
2 tablespoons all-purpose flour
1 cup milk, heated to scalding
½ teaspoon salt
Freshly ground white pepper
 to taste
Pinch freshly ground allspice
1 medium size, ripe avocado,
 peeled and pitted (see note)

2 rounded tablespoons
 minced scallions (green
 parts only)
Dash fresh lime juice
2 egg yolks, at room
 temperature
3 egg whites, at room
 temperature

1 Preheat oven to 375 degrees.

2 Melt butter in medium pot. Add flour and stir to form paste. Do not allow to brown. Add milk to butter mixture and whisk well to blend. Cook over low heat, whisking constantly until mixture is thick and smooth. Stir in salt, white pepper, and allspice. Remove from heat.

3 Puree avocado and scallions in a blender or food processor fitted with a steel blade. Add lime juice. Beat the egg yolks into the avocado mixture. Stir avocado mixture into milk mixture. Set over very low heat and cook, stirring constantly until thickened. Do not allow to come to a boil. Set aside to cool, stirring occasionally so avocado mixture doesn't form a skin.

4 Beat egg whites until stiff. Whisk ¼ of egg whites into avocado mixture to lighten, then fold into whites.

5 Gently spoon into a greased and floured 1½-quart soufflé dish. Place inside a larger pan. Fill the larger pan with hot water to come halfway up the sides of the soufflé dish. Bake for 30 to 45 minutes, until soufflé is lightly browned and barely quivers when the dish is gently moved. Remove from oven and serve immediately.

NOTE *Choose the dark, rough-skinned Hass variety for this souffle; the smooth Fuerte tends to be too rich.*

TURKEY MARSALA

INGREDIENTS

2 slices turkey cutlet (about
  ¼ to ⅓ pound total)
2 tablespoons all-purpose
  flour
½ teaspoon salt
Freshly ground black pepper
  to taste
2 tablespoons butter

1 large or 2 small cloves
  garlic, crushed
¼ cup Marsala wine
¼ cup beef broth

1 Place pieces of turkey between 2 sheets of waxed paper. Pound turkey to ⅛ inch thickness, making sure cutlets are an even thickness. Combine flour, salt, and pepper on a dish. Dust turkey on both sides with flour mixture.

2 Melt butter in a large skillet with the garlic. Add turkey. Sauté over medium-high heat allowing about 2 minutes per side. When turkey is just cooked, remove to a plate and keep warm. Discard garlic.

3 Add Marsala and broth to skillet. Turn heat up high. Scrape up bits from bottom of the skillet. Allow mixture to reduce to a thick, syrupy state (this takes about 5 minutes). Return the turkey to the skillet and turn meat to coat both sides with the Marsala mixture. Serve immediately.

SERVES 1

NOTE *Of course, you can substitute veal for the turkey in this recipe, and the recipe can be doubled.*

LAMB KABOBS

INGREDIENTS

½ pound ground lamb
2 tablespoons fresh, minced
coriander (cilantro)
1 teaspoon minced gingerroot
1 teaspoon minced garlic
½ teaspoon crushed cumin
seeds
½ teaspoon red pepper flakes

Salt and freshly ground black
pepper to taste
Chutney (optional) or yogurt
sauce (see note)

1 Preheat broiler or grill.

2 Combine lamb, coriander, gingerroot, garlic, cumin, red pepper flakes, salt, and pepper to taste. Mix well. Divide in half.

3 Shape each portion into a log and press around a metal skewer to make a 7-inch long sausage. Broil 6 to 8 minutes, turning once. Season with salt and pepper and serve with chutney, if desired.

PHOTO OPPOSITE PAGE 37

NOTE *To make a yogurt sauce, combine the following: ¼ cup plain yogurt; 1 tablespoon minced scallions, green part only; a generous amount of freshly ground black pepper.*
Chill for 1 hour. Spoon the sauce over the cooked kabobs. The recipe can be halved.

BULGUR PILAF

INGREDIENTS

1 tablespoon butter
1 large clove garlic, minced
2 level tablespoons pine nuts
½ cup bulgur (cracked
*   wheat)*
1 cup beef broth
Salt and freshly ground white
*   pepper to taste*

1 Melt butter in medium pot. Sauté garlic and pine nuts over low heat for 3 to 5 minutes, until nuts are lightly browned.

2 Add bulgur and cook, stirring for 1 or 2 minutes, until all the grains are butter coated. Add beef broth and turn heat up to high. Stir once. When mixture begins to boil, reduce heat to low. Cover and simmer mixture for 12 to 15 minutes, until liquid is absorbed and bulgur is tender. Taste and season with salt and white pepper.

PHOTO OPPOSITE PAGE 37

NOTE *Try this preparation for rice as well. The cooking time will remain the same for long-grain rice. Use chicken broth in place of the beef broth when serving pilaf as an accompaniment to plain grilled chicken.*
*   To vary the dish, try the following additions: ¼ cup golden seedless raisins, 2 tablespoons onions that have been sautéed in a little butter, ¼ cup chopped, pitted dates, or ¼ cup cooked vermicelli.*
*   The recipe can be halved.*

POACHED EGGS, ARTICHOKES, AND MAYONNAISE SAUCE

INGREDIENTS

2 medium to large artichokes
1/2 lemon (optional)
2 tablespoons vegetable oil
1 clove garlic, mashed
Dash of lemon juice
Mayonnaise Sauce (recipe
  follows)
2 eggs

1 Trim stems off artichokes. If desired, trim tips off leaves and brush with a cut lemon. Combine oil, garlic, and lemon juice with about 3 quarts water. Bring to boiling. Add artichokes. Reduce heat to low and partially cover. Cook artichokes 45 minutes, or until very tender when pierced with a knife tip.

2 Meanwhile prepare Mayonnaise Sauce and set aside.

3 When artichokes are done, remove from the water and allow to cool to lukewarm. Pull off the tender leaves of 1 artichoke and arrange on 1 serving plate. Remove and discard the fuzzy choke in the center. Then place the artichoke bottom in the center of the leaf arrangement. Repeat with the second artichoke.

4 Poach the 2 eggs or gently fry if that seems easier. The eggs should still have loose yolks. Place 1 egg on top of each artichoke bottom. Spoon the mayonnaise sauce lightly over the leaves and egg. Serve any remaining mayonnaise on the side.

PHOTO OPPOSITE PAGE 69

NOTE *I call this Mayonnaise Sauce because it is slightly looser than a true mayonnaise. It will firm up somewhat if chilled.*

MAYONNAISE SAUCE

INGREDIENTS

1 egg, at room temperature
1 tablespoon lemon juice
Scant 1/4 teaspoon salt
Freshly ground white pepper
  to taste
1/8 teaspoon dry mustard
1/2 cup vegetable oil or 1/4 cup
  vegetable oil and 1/4 cup
  olive oil

1 In blender or food processor equipped with a plastic or steel blade, combine the egg, lemon juice, salt, white pepper, and dry mustard. Process 30 seconds, until smooth.

2 Trickle in the oil in a steady stream until the mixture thickens and becomes smooth.

MAKES ABOUT ¾ CUP

CHAPTER

9

Enjoy some outdoor meals this month. Rather than grabbing a bite in a fast-food restaurant, pack a sandwich in pita bread and eat lunch in a nearby plaza or park. There are two portable lunches to choose from: Swiss, Ham, and Olive Pita Sandwich and Mayonnaise-Chicken Pita. Include a container of fresh strawberries and a sunny day.

Two alternative al fresco lunches—the nearest terrace or porch will do—are Shrimp and Goat Cheese Salad and a loaf of Walnut Bread or Duck and Orange Salad with Corn Muffins.

Vodka and Smoked Salmon Pasta is a luscious, yet light dish. The alcohol in the vodka cooks off, imparting a delicate, smoky flavor. Garlicky Roast Peppers in a vinaigrette dressing will cut some of the richness of the pasta.

Another dish that has the essence, but not the punch, of alcohol is Chicken with Orange and Brandy. If you love the sweet, aromatic seasonings used in Moghul Indian cooking you will enjoy the recipe for Fragrant Brown Rice to be served with the chicken; otherwise prepare the Lemon Rice on page 95. A crisp Green Bean and Blue Cheese Salad is a fine addition to the meal.

SWISS, HAM, AND OLIVE PITA SANDWICH

INGREDIENTS

2 ounces ham, diced
2 ounces Swiss cheese, diced
2 tablespoons chopped
  pimiento-stuffed olives
1 tablespoon chopped celery
2 tablespoons mayonnaise
½ tablespoon prepared
  mustard
1 pita bread

1 In a small bowl, combine ham, cheese, olives, and celery. Stir together mayonnaise and mustard and fold into ham mixture, stirring well.

2 Toast pita bread, if desired. Split in half to form 2 pockets. Open and divide filling between pockets.

SERVES 1

NOTE *I first became intrigued with stuffed sandwiches when I was vacationing in Nice, France, a decade ago. Every morning as I headed to the beach I stopped at a café and picked up a fat, round loaf of bread stuffed with olives, tuna, tomatoes, and lettuce and drizzled with Provençal olive oil and vinegar. Sitting in the sun, I worked my way through this hefty concoction, which was sheer bliss.*

A stuffed sandwich is easy to carry, easy to eat, and certainly filling.

Sandwiches using mayonnaise as a dressing provide some—but not complete—protection against food spoilage. To be safe, I recommend chilling sandwiches and keeping them in a cool place. If this is impossible, substitute a vinaigrette dressing in these two sandwiches. Whisk together 3 to 4 tablespoons olive oil, 1 tablespoon lemon juice or white wine vinegar, and salt and pepper to taste.

OPPOSITE: Pistachio-Coated Fish Fillets with Lemon Butter (page 104).

MAYONNAISE-CHICKEN PITA

INGREDIENTS

*1 cup dry white wine plus ½
 cup water (or 1½ cups
 water)*
1 bay leaf
*2 or 3 white peppercorns,
 crushed*
1 chicken breast half
1 Jerusalem artichoke
*1 rounded tablespoon minced
 red onion*

*¼ teaspoon good-quality
 curry powder*
*3 to 4 tablespoons
 mayonnaise*
*Salt and freshly ground white
 pepper to taste*
1 pita bread

1 Place wine in a small pot with water, bay leaf, and peppercorns. Bring to the boil. Reduce heat to low and add chicken. Cover pot and simmer chicken 20 to 30 minutes, or until it is cooked through. Remove chicken from broth and allow it to cool until it can be touched.

2 Meanwhile, peel and dice artichoke. Combine with onion, curry powder, and mayonnaise. Remove skin from chicken. Tear meat into chunks and add to artichoke mixture. Season with salt and white pepper.

3 Toast pita if desired. Split in half to form 2 pockets. Open and divide filling between pockets.

SERVES 1

NOTE *Instead of a Jerusalem artichoke, a very small, tart apple, peeled or not, could be substituted.*

OPPOSITE: Chicken, Avocado, and Blue Cheese
Salad (page 96).

SHRIMP AND GOAT CHEESE SALAD

INGREDIENTS

*3/4 pound raw shrimp in the
    shell*
*4 rounded tablespoons
    mayonnaise*
*1/2 teaspoon good-quality
    medium-hot paprika*
*Salt and freshly ground white
    pepper to taste*
1/2 cup slivered radishes

*2 ounces mild goat cheese,
    crumbled*
*2 large attractive lettuce
    leaves*

1 Cook shrimp in the shell for 5 minutes. Cool, peel, and devein. If shrimp are large, cut into bite-size pieces. Leave small or medium shrimp as is. Place shrimp in a salad bowl.

2 Combine mayonnaise, paprika, and salt and white pepper. Fold into shrimp. Add radishes and goat cheese. Stir gently. Line 2 salad plates with lettuce. Divide shrimp mixture between plates.

NOTE   *Recipe can be halved.*

For a luncheon, serve the Shrimp and Goat Cheese Salad over avocados. Cut a ripe avocado in half. Peel and remove the pit. Brush lightly with lemon juice to prevent the flesh from browning. Divide the salad between the two halves and garnish the plates with lemon wedges.

There are many goat cheese products to choose from, but I prefer the goat cheese produced in northern California by Laura Chenel.

WALNUT BREAD

INGREDIENTS

1 package active dry yeast
Pinch of sugar
1 cup very warm water
1 teaspoon salt
1½ cups all-purpose flour
1 cup oat flour
2 tablespoons walnut oil
½ cup black walnuts

1 Combine yeast, sugar, and ¼ cup warm water in a cup. Stir and set aside for 10 minutes, until mixture becomes thick.

2 In a large bowl, combine salt, 1 cup all-purpose flour, and the oat flour. Stir well. Pour in yeast mixture, remaining ¾ cup warm water and the oil. Mix well to form a sticky dough. Add the walnuts. Then add more all-purpose flour to reach a dough consistency that can be kneaded (it will probably require 4 tablespoons flour).

3 Turn dough out onto a floured board and knead well for 10 minutes. Place dough in a greased bowl and turn to grease all sides. Cover with a towel and place in a warm spot to rise for 1½ hours.

4 Punch dough down and divide in half. Shape into 2 loaves, each about 7 inches long. Place on greased cookie sheet. Cover with a towel and set aside in a warm place to rise for 1 hour.

5 Preheat oven to 375 degrees. Bake bread for 40 minutes or until it is nicely browned.

6 Cool on a wire rack before cutting. If both breads aren't going to be eaten within the day, wrap one in foil and freeze.

MAKES 2 SMALL LOAVES

VODKA AND SMOKED SALMON PASTA

INGREDIENTS

2 tablespoons butter
4 tablespoons good-quality
  vodka (a smoky flavor is
  desirable)
¾ cup heavy cream
4 ounces smoked salmon,
  chopped
8 ounces fettuccini

1 tablespoon fresh, minced
  parsley
Freshly ground white pepper
  to taste

1 Melt butter in a large skillet. Add vodka and simmer 3 minutes. Add cream and bring to a boil. Cook 3 to 5 minutes, until slightly thickened. Add smoked salmon, reduce heat, and simmer another 5 minutes. Set aside.

2 Cook fettuccini until tender. Drain thoroughly and add to salmon mixture. Sprinkle with parsley and add white pepper. Toss gently, but thoroughly. Serve immediately.

NOTE *Experiment with smoked whitefish or sable in this dish. Purchase 8 ounces of good-quality smoked fish. Remove the skin and bones and break up the fish into bite-size flakes. Add the fish in place of the salmon in the recipe.*

This dish gets a pasty consistency if allowed to stand. It must be served as soon as it is ready.

The recipe can be halved.

GARLICKY ROAST PEPPERS

INGREDIENTS

1 large red or green bell pepper
1/2 teaspoon minced garlic
2 tablespoons sliced,
  pimiento-stuffed olives
1 tablespoon olive oil
1 teaspoon shallot-flavored
  vinegar
Salt and freshly ground black
  pepper to taste

1 Hold pepper over an open flame and turn occasionally until all sides blister and blacken. Put pepper in a plastic bag. Close and set aside for 30 minutes. Peel pepper, core, and cut into strips.

2 Place in a serving bowl. Toss with garlic and olive slices. In a small cup, whisk together oil, vinegar, salt, and pepper. Pour over peppers and set aside for 30 minutes before serving.

NOTE *There are several brands of roast peppers in cans or jars that can be substituted for a quick salad. Buy the smallest quantity possible.*
 For an aromatic flavor, crush 1/2 teaspoon dried oregano between your fingers and sprinkle the herb over the peppers along with the dressing.
 This dish is better if flavored with very little salt, since the olives tend to be salty. Substitute 1 or 2 tablespoons of capers for the olives if you prefer. Plenty of pepper—1/4 to 1/2 teaspoon will enhance the dish.
 This recipe can be halved.

CHICKEN WITH ORANGE AND BRANDY

INGREDIENTS

2 chicken breast halves
1/4 cup all-purpose flour
Salt and freshly ground white
  pepper to taste
2 tablespoons each butter and
  vegetable oil
1/4 cup brandy
1/2 cup orange juice

1/2 teaspoon ground ginger
1 teaspoon grated orange rind
Fragrant Brown Rice (recipe
  follows)

1 Pat chicken dry if damp. Combine flour, 1/2 teaspoon salt, and white pepper to taste on a dinner plate. Roll breasts in flour mixture to coat. Heat together butter and oil in heavy-bottomed skillet. Add chicken pieces and brown well on both sides, about 10 minutes total.

2 Remove chicken and set aside. Pour off fat. Add brandy to skillet over low heat and stir bottom of skillet to get up any browned, flavorful bits. Stir in orange juice and ginger. Add chicken breasts. Cover and simmer 15 minutes or until chicken is cooked through. Stir in orange rind. Season with salt and pepper. Serve over Fragrant Brown Rice.

PHOTO OPPOSITE PAGE 52

NOTE *For one serving, use one chicken breast half, 1 tablespoon each butter and oil, but the same amounts of the remaining ingredients. There will be a little leftover sauce.*

FRAGRANT BROWN RICE

INGREDIENTS

1 tablespoon vegetable oil
2 shallots, minced
¼ teaspoon black caraway
seeds (see note)
1 small cinnamon stick (2 to
3 inches)
2 whole cloves
2 allspice berries
1 bay leaf

½ cup brown rice
1 cup chicken broth
Salt and freshly ground black
pepper to taste

1 Heat oil in small saucepan. Add shallots and sauté 2 to 3 minutes. Add caraway seeds, cinnamon stick, cloves, allspice, and bay leaf and sauté 2 minutes, stirring constantly.

2 Add brown rice and stir 1 to 2 minutes, until grains are shiny. Add chicken broth and bring to a boil. Reduce heat to low, cover the pan and cook rice 45 to 50 minutes. Then, set aside 5 minutes, covered. Remove cinnamon stick and bay leaf. If possible, also remove cloves and allspice. Season with salt and pepper.

PHOTO OPPOSITE PAGE 52

NOTE *Black caraway seeds, which are black, aromatic chips, are also called Russian caraway seeds. They are sold in Polish, Russian, and Indian food stores.*

MAY

GREEN BEAN AND BLUE CHEESE SALAD

INGREDIENTS

1 tablespoon blue cheese
1 tablespoon unsalted butter
¼ pound green beans
2 to 3 tablespoons vegetable
   oil
1 tablespoon shallot-flavored
   white wine vinegar

Salt and freshly ground white
   pepper to taste
2 tablespoons minced parsley
   for a garnish

1 Cream together the blue cheese and butter and set aside at room temperature. Don't allow butter to melt or the dish will taste oily.

2 Cut tips off green beans. Wash. Cut beans into 1-inch pieces. Steam for 5 minutes, or until tender, but still crunchy. Set aside.

3 Whisk together 2 tablespoons oil, vinegar, salt, and pepper in a bowl. Taste and add additional oil if desired. The dressing should be slightly more tart than the usual vinaigrette.

4 To serve, arrange beans on 2 salad plates. Top each with a small mound of the butter-cheese mixture. Drizzle oil and vinegar mixture over both servings. Sprinkle with parsley.

NOTE *Recipe can be halved.*

JUNE

CHAPTER

10

Fish are an especially good foundation for summer meals because they are low in calories, light, and cook quickly.

The first fish suggestion for June is an herbed Fish Stew similar to the California cioppino. Make the tomato base first. It will keep well in the refrigerator up to three days or in the freezer for several months. Cook the fish briefly in the tomato base just before serving. Spoon the Fish Stew over Lemon Rice for an entree.

Chicken, Avocado, and Blue Cheese Salad is a popular warm-weather combination. Coriander gives this salad a fresh, slightly anise flavor. To contrast the sharp salad taste, assemble a side dish of Tempura Vegetables with a delicate flour coating and a pungent Tempura Sauce for dipping. If you add a few raw shrimp or fish cubes to the vegetable selection for frying, you've got a nourishing entree.

The second fish menu is Salmon with Scallion Sauce and an accompanying Snow Pea-Tomato Sauté.

Chicken with Oregano is a staple on Greek restaurant menus. The refreshing taste of lemon combined with the potency of garlic and oregano could make it a classic in your kitchen as well. Potato salad gets lively new flavor with the addition of watercress and sour cream to the dressing.

FISH STEW

INGREDIENTS

2 tablespoons olive oil
1 small green bell pepper, diced
1 small onion, peeled and
   diced
1 large clove garlic, minced
1 can (about 14 ounces)
   stewed tomatoes
1 tablespoon tomato paste
1 to 1½ teaspoons fresh,
   minced basil

½ teaspoon dried oregano
1 bay leaf
Salt and freshly ground black
   pepper to taste
¼ cup dry red wine
½ pound fish fillets or steaks
   (halibut or scrod)
1 teaspoon fresh lemon juice
Lemon Rice (recipe follows)

1 Heat oil in medium pot. Add green pepper. Sauté in oil 5 minutes. Add onion and garlic and sauté an additional 5 minutes. Add tomatoes, tomato paste, basil, oregano, bay leaf, salt, pepper, and red wine. Simmer 15 minutes, stirring occasionally.

2 Cut fish into 1-inch chunks. Add to stew mixture. Cover pot and simmer 5 to 10 minutes, or until fish loses its transparency. Stir in lemon juice. Spoon some Lemon Rice into 2 bowls. Ladle the fish stew over the rice and serve.

PHOTO OPPOSITE PAGE 53

LEMON RICE

INGREDIENTS

1 tablespoon butter
½ cup rice
¼ teaspoon salt
1 cup water
2 pieces lemon peel (about 1
 inch each)
1 tablespoon fresh, minced
 parsley

1 Melt butter in a small pot. Add rice and stir to coat all the grains. Add salt, water, and lemon peel. Bring to a boil.

2 Reduce heat and cover tightly. Simmer about 12 to 15 minutes, until liquid is absorbed and rice is tender. Remove lemon peel and discard. Stir parsley into rice.

CHICKEN, AVOCADO, AND BLUE CHEESE SALAD

INGREDIENTS

*2 cups dry white wine plus 1
  cup water (or 3 cups water)*
2 bay leaves
5 peppercorns
2 chicken breast halves
3 cups torn lettuce (Bibb or Boston)
*1 avocado, peeled, pitted,
  and cubed*
*¼ cup fresh coriander leaves
  (cilantro)*

1 rib celery, sliced
*1 scallion, green part only,
  sliced*
5 tablespoons olive oil
2 tablespoons herb vinegar
*1½ teaspoons Dijon-style
  mustard*
*Salt and freshly ground white
  pepper to taste*
½ cup crumbled blue cheese

1 Combine wine, water, bay leaves, and peppercorns in a medium pot. Bring to a boil. Add chicken breast halves and reduce heat. Cover with lid slightly ajar and simmer about 20 to 30 minutes. Remove chicken from broth and allow to cool. Discard broth.

2 While chicken is cooking combine lettuce, avocado, coriander, celery, and scallion in a large salad bowl. Tear chicken meat off the bones in bite-size pieces. Add to salad.

3 In a small bowl, whisk together the oil, vinegar, mustard, salt, and white pepper. Pour over the salad and toss well. Top with crumbled blue cheese.

PHOTO OPPOSITE PAGE 85

TEMPURA VEGETABLES

INGREDIENTS

2 cups prepared vegetables
  (sliced mushrooms, sliced
  zucchini, broccoli and
  cauliflower broken into
  small flowerets, green
  beans cut into 1-inch
  lengths, and carrots sliced
  on the diagonal ⅛ inch
  thick)

Oil for deep-fat frying
1 egg yolk
¾ cup ice cold water
Salt to taste
⅔ cup all-purpose flour
Tempura Sauce (recipe
  follows)

1 Select any or all the vegetables listed. If using broccoli, cauliflower, green beans, or carrots blanch briefly first (dip in boiling hot water for 1 minute, then remove, rinse under cold water, drain and pat dry). Have all vegetables ready before preparing batter.

2 Heat about 1 inch of oil to 375 degrees in deep fryer or high-sided skillet.

3 Whisk together egg yolk, ice cold water, salt, and flour until no large lumps remain. There may be some small lumps. Dip vegetables into batter, draining off excess and ease into oil. Fry until golden on one side, turn over and fry second side. This should take less than 5 minutes total. Don't crowd pan, but work fast as batter tends to thicken. Drain fried vegetables on paper toweling. There may be excess batter which should be discarded.

4 While vegetables are frying, prepare Tempura Sauce. Divide between 2 small cups. Divide vegetables into 2 portions and serve each with a small cup for dipping.

PHOTO OPPOSITE PAGE 101

TEMPURA SAUCE

INGREDIENTS

1 tablespoon soy sauce
1½ teaspoons brown sugar
⅛ teaspoon ground ginger
½ teaspoon red wine vinegar
½ to 1 teaspoon saki or dry
  Sherry

1 Combine soy sauce, brown sugar, ginger, vinegar, and saki or dry Sherry.

2 Stir well to dissolve sugar.

MAKES ABOUT 2 TABLESPOONS SAUCE

SALMON WITH SCALLION SAUCE

INGREDIENTS

*1 cup Fume Blanc or similar
  white wine*
5 to 6 peppercorns
2 bay leaves
*2 salmon steaks (each about
  1 inch thick; total weight
  about ¾ pound)*
½ cup heavy cream

1 tablespoon minced scallions
1 tablespoon butter
Salt to taste

1 In large skillet, bring to a boil the wine, peppercorns, and bay leaves. Add salmon steaks. Reduce heat to medium and cover skillet. Cook fish 10 minutes, turning over after 5 minutes. Remove salmon from skillet and keep warm. Remove and discard peppercorns and bay leaves. Increase heat and reduce liquid to 1 to 2 tablespoons. Add cream and scallions.

2 Reduce heat to low and cook until mixture bubbles and thickens slightly, about 5 minutes. Remove from heat. Cut butter into slivers and add to sauce, rotating skillet to incorporate. Season sauce lightly with salt. Return salmon to skillet. Spoon sauce over salmon and heat through. Serve immediately.

NOTE *Recipe can be halved.*

JUNE

SNOW PEA-TOMATO SAUTÉ

INGREDIENTS

1 tablespoon vegetable oil
1 tablespoon butter
4 ounces fresh snow peas
1 shallot, minced
1 cup cherry tomatoes
½ tablespoon light soy sauce
Freshly ground black pepper
*   to taste*

1 Heat oil and butter in a medium skillet. While oil is heating, steam peas for 2 to 3 minutes. Add peas, shallot, and cherry tomatoes to skillet, and cook over medium heat, stirring constantly, yet gently, for about 2 minutes.

2 Add soy sauce. Stir and cook for 1 minute. Season with freshly ground pepper. Serve immediately.

NOTE *Turn this dish into a salad with an interesting honey and poppy seed dressing.*

Cook the peas, shallot, and tomatoes according to the directions and set aside. Omit the second step, then prepare the dressing with the following ingredients: 1 tablespoon honey, 1½ tablespoons lemon juice, 1 tablespoon vegetable oil, ½ teaspoon poppy seeds, and salt and freshly ground black pepper to taste.

Stir together honey and lemon juice in a small cup until the honey dissolves. Add oil, poppy seeds, salt, and pepper to taste. Pour part of the dressing over the salad and toss gently. Add additional dressing to taste.

The recipe can be halved. If making the salad variation prepare the full amount and refrigerate the leftovers.

OPPOSITE: Cheese, Tomato, and Caper Salad
(page 109).

CHICKEN WITH OREGANO

INGREDIENTS

2 tablespoons mild olive oil
2 tablespoons lemon juice
1 small clove garlic, minced
¼ teaspoon dried, crushed oregano
Salt and freshly ground white
  pepper to taste
1 chicken breast half

1 Combine oil and lemon juice in medium bowl. Add garlic, oregano, ½ teaspoon salt, and white pepper. Stir well. Add chicken and turn to coat all sides. Set aside to marinate at room temperature 1 hour, turning occasionally.

2 Preheat oven to 400 degrees.

3 Place rack over a cookie sheet and arrange chicken on rack (or place directly on shallow pan). Roast for 30 to 40 minutes, basting every 10 minutes with remaining marinade. Season with salt and pepper. Serve hot or tepid.

SERVES 1

NOTE *Chicken can also be cooked outdoors on the grill. Baste often with marinade.*
   The combination of lemon juice and oregano is marvelous on a whole roasted chicken as well. Here is an adaptation of the above recipe:

   1 broiler-fryer chicken, about 3 pounds
   Salt and freshly ground white pepper to taste
   1 tablespoon butter or olive oil
   ½ lemon
   1 teaspoon dried, crushed oregano

Wash chicken inside and out with cold water and pat dry. Season cavity and outside of chicken with salt and pepper. Place chicken on a rack over a cookie sheet (or place directly on a shallow pan). Cut butter into small pieces and place on chicken. If you're using the oil, drizzle it over the chicken. Squeeze the lemon juice over the chicken and sprinkle with oregano.
   Cook in a preheated 400-degree oven for 45 minutes to 1 hour, or until the chicken is a dark, golden brown.

OPPOSITE: Tempura Vegetables (page 97).

POTATO-WATERCRESS SALAD

INGREDIENTS

3 small to medium new
    potatoes (³/₄ pound total)
¹/₂ cup watercress leaves
¹/₄ cup minced red onion
2 rounded tablespoons
    mayonnaise
2 tablespoons sour cream
1 teaspoon prepared mustard
Salt and freshly ground black
    pepper to taste

1 Cook potatoes in water to cover until tender, about 30 minutes. Drain well. Peel and quarter.

2 Mix potato pieces with watercress leaves and onion. Mix together mayonnaise, sour cream, and mustard. Stir into potato mixture. Season with salt and pepper.

NOTE *Few people can resist the lower prices of potatoes purchased in 5-pound sacks. To store those extra potatoes, keep them in a cool, dry place. They should not be refrigerated, nor should they be stored next to onions or they will sprout and turn bad.*

Check the potatoes every few days. If they are softening, use immediately.

Recipe can be halved.

JULY

CHAPTER

11

Fresh corn-on-the-cob, ripe tomatoes, lush eggplant, and fragrant basil are all a delightful part of July's meals.

Now that pistachios are in good supply and reasonably priced, use the green-fleshed nut for cooking as well as snacking. Serve Pistachio-Coated Fish Fillets with Lemon Butter and Spicy Corn for a sophisticated, yet easy summer meal.

When the heat's on, cool off with Scallop Salad. Choose tender bay scallops to marinate in lime juice and seasonings. The acid in the juice firms up the scallops so no cooking is needed. Make Eggplant Steaks to go with the salad.

Fresh, farm-raised mussels are one of the least expensive seafood choices available. But don't be swayed by price alone. Mussels are meaty, quick cooking, and versatile. In the recipe that follows mussels are used in place of clams in the pasta dish, Linguini with Mussels Sauce. Serve Cheese, Tomato, and Caper Salad as a first course.

Summer's Sunday brunches should feature bold, gutsy-flavored foods, not the bland, rich dishes that are a solace during winter. Huevos Rancheros is a potent choice for a mid-day meal. Create a Southwestern platter with the eggs, tortillas, salsa, and Spanish Rice. Serve lemonade, sangria, or iced tea as the beverage.

PISTACHIO-COATED FISH FILLETS WITH LEMON BUTTER

INGREDIENTS

7 tablespoons clarified butter
12 ounces red snapper,
  flounder, or other thin fish
  fillets, in 2 portions
4 ounces natural pistachios,
  shelled and minced
1 teaspoon grated lemon rind
2 teaspoons lemon juice
Salt and freshly ground white
  pepper to taste

1 Brush 2 teaspoons of the clarified butter on the skinless side of each fish fillet. Press half the pistachios onto the buttered side of each fish fillet.

2 Heat 3 tablespoons clarified butter in a large skillet over medium heat. Ease fish fillets into skillet. Cook 3 to 4 minutes, occasionally loosening fish with a spatula if necessary. Carefully turn fish over and cook second side 1 to 2 minutes.

3 Meanwhile, heat remaining clarified butter over low heat in a small skillet. Add lemon rind and juice. Ease fish onto 2 serving platters. Season with salt and white pepper. Pour all or part of lemon butter over the fish. Serve immediately.

PHOTO OPPOSITE PAGE 84

NOTE *Recipe can be halved.*

SPICY CORN

INGREDIENTS

1 large ear of corn
3 tablespoons butter
1 teaspoon red pepper flakes
¹/₂ teaspoon cumin seeds
¹/₂ teaspoon salt

1 Preheat oven to 425 degrees.

2 Husk corn. Mash together butter, red pepper flakes, cumin, and salt. Place each ear of corn on a sheet of heavy-duty foil. Spread evenly with butter mixture and fold up foil to seal, leaving some air space. Roast for 15 minutes. Be careful when opening packet; it's hot.

NOTE *July and August are peak months for fresh corn, so there's no reason to not get your fill. Fortunately this vegetable is usually sold by the ear, rather than in packages, so you can select as much as you need.*

Pull back the husk and examine the kernels. They should be firm and plump, but not too large, as this often indicates a starchy taste. Avoid kernels with large spaces between the rows, and of course, look for insect infestation.

Store the corn, unhusked, in the refrigerator, but plan to use it within 2 days of purchase. The longer corn is held, the more its "sugar" is lost.

The recipe can be halved.

SCALLOP SALAD

INGREDIENTS

½ pound bay scallops
1 small red onion, peeled and
  thinly sliced
Juice of 3 limes (⅓ cup lime
  juice)
Salt and freshly ground white
  pepper to taste
½ teaspoon crushed red
  pepper flakes

2 tablespoons fresh, chopped
  coriander (cilantro)
Olive oil
1 medium tomato, seeded
  and coarsely chopped
2 large, attractive lettuce
  leaves

1 Drain scallops. Rinse under cold water and pat dry. Place in a glass or enamel bowl. Separate onion slices into rings and add to scallops. Combine lime juice, salt, white pepper, red pepper flakes, and coriander. Pour over scallop mixture.

2 Place in a cool spot and let stand about 2 hours, turning or stirring occasionally. When ready to serve, spoon out half the lime juice. Stir in ¼ to ⅓ cup olive oil. Stir in tomato chunks. Divide between 2 lettuce-lined plates. Serve at room temperature.

NOTE *The acid of the lime juice pickles the scallops, so no cooking is necessary. However, if the scallops are kept in the acid too long they will become mushy.*
  The recipe can be halved.

EGGPLANT STEAKS

INGREDIENTS

1 eggplant (1 pound)
Salt to taste
1 clove garlic, peeled
2 tablespoons butter
2 tablespoons vegetable oil
½ teaspoon dried oregano
Freshly ground black pepper
    to taste

1 Cut top and stem ends off eggplant. Do not peel. Cut into 4 slices. Place on a platter. Sprinkle generously with salt and set aside for 1 hour. Brush salt and eggplant juices off the eggplant slices. Place eggplant on an oiled sheet of foil on a cookie sheet.

2 Preheat oven to 400 degrees.

3 Mash garlic with ¼ teaspoon salt to form a pulp. Combine garlic pulp, butter, and oil in a small skillet. Cook, stirring occasionally only until butter melts and foams. Pour over eggplant slices. Crush oregano between fingers and sprinkle over eggplant.

4 Bake for 25 to 30 minutes until eggplant is tender. Sprinkle with pepper. Gently ease onto plates so eggplant doesn't tear. Serve hot or tepid.

NOTE *To make an entree out of this eggplant side dish, bake the eggplant according to the directions. Then lay a slice of mozzarella cheese over each eggplant slice. Return to the oven for 2 or 3 minutes, or until the cheese just melts. Serve immediately.*

LINGUINI WITH MUSSELS SAUCE

INGREDIENTS

1 pound mussels
Cornmeal
1 cup dry white wine
2 bay leaves
2 tablespoons butter
1 tablespoon olive oil
1 tablespoon vegetable oil
2 teaspoons minced garlic
4 tablespoons fresh, minced
  Italian parsley

6 ounces linguini
Salt and plenty of freshly
  ground white pepper to
  taste

1 Clean mussels, scraping off any dirt from shells and pulling off beards (the scraggly, hairy part) with a sharp knife.

2 Place mussels in a bowl with cold water to cover. Stir in a tablespoon or two of cornmeal and set aside for 1 hour. Discard water mixture. Rinse mussels under cold running water and discard any that won't close.

3 Heat wine in medium pot. When it boils, add bay leaves and mussels. Cover and cook over medium heat 3 to 4 minutes, shaking pot. Shells should open; discard any that remain shut. Set aside until cool enough to handle. Pluck meat from shells and set aside. Discard shells.

4 Strain liquid through a layer of cheesecloth. Return liquid to pot and reduce to ½ cup.

5 Meanwhile, heat together butter, olive oil, and vegetable oil. Add garlic and cook over low heat 5 minutes. Coarsely chop mussels and add to butter mixture along with parsley and reduced liquid.

6 Cook linguini until just tender. Drain well and spoon into a serving bowl. Pour mussels mixture over linguini and toss well. Season lightly with salt and generously with white pepper and toss again. Serve immediately.

CHEESE, TOMATO, AND CAPER SALAD

INGREDIENTS

1 medium tomato
1 ounce Mozzarella cheese
1 tablespoon fresh, minced
 basil
1 tablespoon olive oil
½ teaspoon white wine
 vinegar

1 teaspoon small capers (with
 a little of the brine)
Salt and freshly ground black
 pepper to taste

1 Slice tomato and arrange on a salad plate. Cut cheese into 1-inch sticks. Sprinkle over tomato slices. Sprinkle basil on top.

2 Whisk together olive oil and vinegar. Add capers. Taste and season with salt and pepper. Pour over salad.

PHOTO OPPOSITE PAGE 100. SERVES 1

NOTE *This is still another way of combining tomatoes, basil, and cheese, a dish that has become a summer classic. There has been a massive education program started by tomato growers to teach consumers how to handle tomatoes. Their advice is to* never *refrigerate tomatoes. This kills the ripening process and flattens the taste.*

If you've been unhappy with tomato flavor, see how much better it is when the tomatoes are kept out of the refrigerator.

And keep that tip in mind when making Cheese, Tomato, and Caper Salad. Serve the dish at room temperature, not chilled.

Although the entree is for 2, I made this a single serving salad because it does double duty as a refreshing light lunch for 1. The recipe can easily be doubled.

HUEVOS RANCHEROS

INGREDIENTS

2 small jalapeño peppers,
  seeded and minced
¼ cup minced onion (1 small onion)
1 cup peeled, seeded, and
  chopped plum tomatoes, or
  drained, seeded and
  chopped canned tomatoes
4 tablespoons tomato paste
½ teaspoon ground cumin

Salt and freshly ground black
  pepper to taste
1 tablespoon water
Spanish Rice (recipe follows)
¼ cup vegetable oil
2 large corn tortillas
4 eggs
1 cup shredded Monterey
  Jack cheese

1 Preheat broiler.

2 Combine jalapeño peppers, onion, tomatoes, tomato paste, cumin, salt, pepper, and water in a blender or food processor fitted with a steel blade. Blend until only slightly chunky. Remove to a small saucepan. Keep over low heat.

3 Prepare Spanish Rice. While it simmers prepare the rest of the dish.

4 Heat oil in a large skillet. Cook tortillas, one at a time, allowing about 30 seconds per side. Tortillas should remain slightly flexible. Drain on paper towels. Then place 2 tortillas on 2 heat-proof plates.

5 Pour off all but 2 tablespoons oil. Gently ease eggs into skillet and cook until whites are firm, but yolks are still soft and runny. Remove eggs. Place 2 on top of each tortilla. Divide pepper-tomato sauce, spooning half over each plate. Sprinkle ½ cup cheese over each portion.

6 Place plates under broiler until cheese melts, about 1 minute. Spoon Spanish Rice onto each plate and serve immediately.

NOTE *Recipe can be halved.*

SPANISH RICE

INGREDIENTS

*1 small green pepper, seeded
and diced*
*1 plum tomato, peeled,
seeded and diced*
*¼ cup minced onion (1 small
onion)*
2 tablespoons vegetable oil
½ cup rice

1 cup chicken broth
*Salt and freshly ground white
pepper to taste*

1 Sauté green pepper, tomato, and onion in oil for 5 minutes in medium pot. Add rice, stir to coat and sauté, stirring frequently for 2 to 3 minutes.

2 Add chicken broth and bring to a boil. Cover, reduce heat to low and simmer 12 minutes or until rice is tender. Season with salt and white pepper to taste.

NOTE *I was first introduced to this breakfast dish at the La Fonda Hotel in Santa Fe, New Mexico, last year. I ordered it for an 8 a.m. meal and was stunned when the waiter brought in a huge platter with huevos rancheros, Spanish rice, refried beans, salsa, warm tortillas, and butter. This was enough to last me until dinner.*

I'm sharing a modified version of this meal. However, for authenticity, prepare the refried beans that follow as well.

Recipe can be halved.

REFRIED BEANS

INGREDIENTS

1 cup pinto beans
2 cups water
2 tablespoons bacon fat
1 clove garlic, minced
1 shallot, or very small
   onion, minced
Salt and freshly ground black
   pepper to taste

¼ cup grated Monterey Jack
   cheese
¼ cup grated Cheddar cheese

1 Place beans in a pot with water. Bring to a boil, cover, and boil 1 minute. Remove from heat. Let beans stand, covered, in the hot water for 1 hour. Then return to the heat and simmer about 1½ hours or until the beans are tender. Check the pot occasionally and add more water as the beans begin to dry.

2 Heat the bacon fat in a large skillet. Sauté garlic and shallot or onion over low heat 5 minutes.

3 Spoon out 1 cup of beans and a little of the cooking liquid. Add to the skillet. Mash with a fork until the mixture is pulpy. Cook over low heat for a few minutes. Repeat with more beans and liquid until all the beans are used.

4 Season with salt and pepper. Sprinkle on both cheeses and allow to melt in. Spoon onto plates to serve.

SERVES 4

NOTE *You'll probably prefer to make this dish in advance. It will keep up to 2 days in the refrigerator. Reheat with an additional tablespoon bacon fat and sprinkle on cheese when reheating.*

CHAPTER

12 By August the profusion of summer produce, at first welcome, becomes overwhelming. This month's menus suggest new ways to use such plentiful vegetables as zucchini, corn, and tomatoes.

Make corn fritters using fresh corn-on-the-cob. Dip the fritters in a ginger, cinnamon, and maple syrup sauce. Sausage Patties, made from scratch, are a robust accompaniment.

Leeks are often used as a flavoring in soups or stews. But see how good the mild, onion flavor of the leek is as starring ingredient in a salad with mustard-vinaigrette dressing. Sautéed Trout With Bacon is a great catch for the main course.

Panzanella—bread salad—with fresh herbs, onion, tomato, and celery, is so satisfying you may find yourself saving stale bread so you can make the recipe over and over. Teriyaki Round Steak with its sweet-smoky flavor rounds out the meal.

Beets and Berries is perhaps the most unusual ingredient combination in this book, and perhaps the biggest surprise. Cook tender sweet beets and flavor with ginger, vinegar, orange juice, and brown sugar. Then toss with plump, ripe blueberries. A Zucchini and Onion Omelet is the entree.

CORN FRITTERS WITH GINGER-CINNAMON SAUCE

INGREDIENTS

1 tablespoon grated
    gingerroot
¼ cup maple syrup
1 stick (2 inches) cinnamon
2 ears corn
Oil for deep-fat frying
½ cup sifted all-purpose flour
1 teaspoon sugar
½ teaspoon baking powder

½ teaspoon salt
1 egg
¼ cup milk

1 Combine gingerroot, maple syrup, and cinnamon stick in small pot. Cook over lowest heat possible for 15 minutes, stirring occasionally. Discard cinnamon. Strain liquid into a serving cup, pressing as much syrup as possible from the ginger. Set aside.

2 Husk the corn. Place it in a medium pot of cold water. Cover and allow the water to come to a boil. Remove from heat. Remove corn from water. Take a sharp paring knife and, starting at the top of the cob, slice down, close to the cob, removing all the corn kernels. Repeat until the cob is clean. Repeat with the second ear. This should yield about ¾ cup corn. A little more or less won't matter.

3 Set corn aside. Preheat 1 inch of oil to 375 degrees in a heavy-bottomed skillet.

4 Sift together flour, sugar, baking powder, and salt. Stir in egg and milk. Stir in corn. Drop heaping tablespoonfuls of batter into the hot oil, being sure not to crowd. Cook for about 2 minutes on one side, until a deep golden color, then turn over and cook the second side.

5 Remove to paper towel-lined plate to drain. Serve with warm ginger-cinnamon sauce. Season with additional salt if desired.

MAKES ABOUT 8 TO 10 FRITTERS

SAUSAGE PATTIES

INGREDIENTS

½ pound ground pork
¼ teaspoon salt
¼ teaspoon freshly ground
  black pepper
1½ teaspoons fresh, minced
  or ½ to ¾ teaspoon dried
  sage, crumbled

¼ to ½ teaspoon fresh,
  minced or ⅛ teaspoon
  dried, crumbled marjoram
2 tablespoons vegetable oil

1 Combine pork, salt, pepper, sage, and marjoram. Chill 1 to 3 hours, for flavors to develop.

2 Shape into 4 patties. Heat oil in a large skillet. Cook meat on both sides, allowing 5 minutes per side. Cook meat thoroughly, but don't press down with a spatula or patties will be dry.

NOTE *Once you discover how easy it is to make sausages from scratch you may never bother with prepared ones again. Many commercial sausages are made with additional fat for a less expensive product and preservatives for longer shelf life. This recipe uses neither.*

Sage is a traditional herb for pork sausages, but you may like some others. Try red pepper flakes, caraway, or cumin for a change. Mix in about ¼ cup minced green pepper or a tablespoon or two of grated Parmesan cheese for new flavors.

Although this recipe can be halved, I doubt that a single will have any problems using the entire amount.

SAUTÉED TROUT WITH BACON

INGREDIENTS

4 bacon strips
½ cup milk
2 trout (about 8 ounces each)
½ cup cornmeal
Dash of cayenne pepper
Salt and freshly ground white
  pepper to taste
¼ cup vegetable oil
1 lemon, cut in wedges

1 Fry bacon in large skillet until crisp. Drain and set aside. Do not discard fat.

2 Pour milk into a pie plate. Soak trout for 10 minutes, turning occasionally. Place cornmeal on a dinner plate. Combine with cayenne, salt, and white pepper. Remove trout from milk and coat fish on both sides with cornmeal. Let rest for a minute or two so coating better adheres to fish.

3 Meanwhile, add vegetable oil to bacon fat in skillet and heat over medium heat. Ease fish into skillet. Cook about 10 to 12 minutes, turning over once during cooking time (when fish is nicely browned on one side, turn to cook other side). Remove from skillet and ease onto 2 serving plates.

4 Crumble reserved bacon and sprinkle over trout. Garnish each plate with lemon wedges.

NOTE *Recipe can be halved. Instead of bacon, you can cook the trout in a combination of 4 tablespoons butter and ¼ cup vegetable oil.*

OPPOSITE: Sautéed Trout with Bacon.

LEEKS WITH MUSTARD DRESSING

INGREDIENTS

4 firm, large leeks
½ cup dry white wine
½ cup water
5 tablespoons olive oil
2 tablespoons balsamic or red
*   wine vinegar*

1 teaspoon coarse-grained
*   mustard*
Salt and freshly ground white
*   pepper to taste*

1 Cut stem ends off leeks. Cut off green parts. Depending on size of leeks, there will be 2 to 4 inches of white. Cut leeks in half vertically. Rinse well in cold water to remove dirt. You may discard tough outer leaves if desired.

2 Place white wine and water in skillet with a lid. Bring mixture to a boil. Add leeks. Reduce heat to low and cover skillet. Simmer 15 to 20 minutes or until leeks are tender. Remove from heat but let sit in liquid while preparing dressing.

3 In a bowl, whisk together oil and vinegar. Stir in mustard. Season with salt and white pepper. Drain leeks. Add to the dressing. Toss gently but well. Set aside for at least 30 minutes. Serve at room temperature.

NOTE *Recipe can be halved.*

OPPOSITE: Rock Cornish Hens with
Fruited Cornbread Stuffing (page 128).

PANZANELLA

INGREDIENTS

2 cups day-old Italian bread
  cubes (about 1 inch in
  diameter)
1 teaspoon minced fresh
  oregano or ½ teaspoon
  dried
1½ teaspoons minced fresh
  basil
1 clove garlic, minced

1 small red onion, minced
1 medium tomato, diced
1 celery stalk, diced
1 tablespoon lemon juice
3½ tablespoons olive oil
Salt and freshly ground black
  pepper to taste

1 Soak bread in just enough water to cover for 15 minutes. Squeeze dry. Place in a bowl. Add oregano, basil, garlic, red onion, tomato, and celery.

2 Whisk together lemon juice, olive oil, salt, and pepper to taste and pour over bread mixture. Toss well.

NOTE *Since this is such a sturdy dish, it makes a fine picnic salad. Make the dish up to 24 hours in advance and store in a cool place, but not the refrigerator.*
Double or triple the recipe for large gatherings. It's a dish that goes fast.
The recipe can be halved.

TERIYAKI ROUND STEAK

INGREDIENTS

*½ pound round steak,
  trimmed of fat*
1 clove garlic, minced
2½ tablespoons teriyaki sauce
1 tablespoon plum wine
¼ teaspoon sesame oil
*¼ teaspoon onion juice (see
  note)*

*1 small red chili, minced
  (seeds and all)*
*Salt and freshly ground black
  pepper to taste*

1 Freeze steak just until very firm. Slice across grain into ¼-inch thick pieces. Combine garlic, teriyaki sauce, wine, oil, onion juice, red chili, salt, and pepper in a glass or enamel bowl. Add steak and toss well. Set aside in cool place to marinate for 1 to 2 hours.

2 Preheat broiler.

3 Line a cookie sheet with foil. Place the meat on the foil and brush generously with marinade. Place meat about 5 inches from heat. Broil about 3 minutes on the first side. Turn meat over and brush again with marinade. Broil 1 more minute.

NOTE *To get ¼ teaspoon onion juice, grate enough onion to yield one heaping tablespoonful. Place in cheesecloth and squeeze out the juice. This recipe can also be done on an outdoor grill.*

BEETS AND BERRIES

INGREDIENTS

4 small to medium beets
1 teaspoon grated gingerroot
3 tablespoons white wine
vinegar
1 tablespoon fresh orange
juice
1 teaspoon grated orange rind
3 tablespoons brown sugar

Salt and freshly ground black
pepper to taste
½ cup blueberries

1 Wash beets and trim off any stems. Place in a pot with water to cover. Bring to a boil, reduce heat and simmer 20 to 30 minutes, until beets are fork-tender. Pour off water and set beets aside until cool enough to handle.

2 Peel off beet skins and cut beets into small dice (about the size of the berries). Combine gingerroot, vinegar, orange juice and rind, brown sugar, salt, and pepper. Pour over beets and toss well.

3 Set aside for 15 minutes to allow beets to absorb dressing. When serving toss in blueberries.

NOTE *Recipe can be halved.*

ZUCCHINI AND ONION OMELET

INGREDIENTS

2 tablespoons butter, divided
1/2 cup thinly sliced zucchini
1/4 cup minced onion
2 eggs
1 tablespoon heavy cream or
  half-and-half
1 rounded teaspoon fresh,
  minced chervil or parsley

1/2 teaspoon fresh, minced or
  1/8 to 1/4 teaspoon dried,
  crushed thyme
Salt and freshly ground white
  pepper to taste

1 Melt 1 tablespoon butter in medium skillet. Sauté zucchini and onion until tender, about 5 to 8 minutes. Spoon zucchini and onion into a bowl and set aside. Keep warm.

2 Wipe out skillet. Melt remaining butter in skillet. Whisk together eggs, cream or half-and-half, chervil or parsley, thyme, salt, and white pepper. Pour into skillet. Cook over medium heat, occasionally lifting up edges of omelet to allow uncooked portion to flow under and cook. Keep omelet loose from pan.

3 When top is creamy and slightly underdone, sprinkle on cooked zucchini and onion. Gently fold omelet in half and ease onto serving plate.

SERVES 1

NOTE *It's all too easy to relegate an omelet to the breakfast table. The French however, consider the dish appropriate to any meal and, indeed, nothing could be more pleasurable than a well-made omelet, some crusty bread, and a glass of Chablis.*

Use the basic technique here, but substitute one of the following for the zucchini to expand your omelet repertoire: 1/2 cup thinly sliced mushrooms; 1/2 cup cubed, peeled, and seeded tomatoes; 1/2 cup peeled and cubed eggplant; or 1/2 cup diced green or red bell peppers.

SNOW PEAS AND CRISP NOODLES

INGREDIENTS

4 ounces snow peas
3 tablespoons vegetable oil
1 cup rice noodles
1 small red chili, cut in half
   and seeded
1 tablespoon soy sauce
2 tablespoons chicken broth

$1/4$ teaspoon cornstarch
Freshly ground white pepper
   to taste

1 Trim tips off snow peas. Bring a medium pot of water to the boil. Add peas and blanch for 1 minute. Remove the peas from the water and rinse under cold water to stop the cooking. Pat dry.

2 Meanwhile, heat oil in a wok or skillet over high heat. Separate noodles into strands and add to the wok. Cook over high heat, stirring constantly until noodles puff and faintly brown. This takes about 30 seconds. Remove and set aside on paper-towel–lined plate to drain. Add chili halves to oil and cook for 30 seconds. Remove and discard.

3 Combine soy sauce, chicken broth, and cornstarch and set aside.

4 Add peas to the oil and stir. Cook over high heat 1 minute. Pour soy sauce mixture into the wok with the peas and cook an additional minute, until the sauce thickens. Spoon the peas and sauce into a serving bowl. Add the noodles; toss gently but well. Season with pepper. Serve immediately.

NOTE *Rice noodles are available in the oriental sections of supermarkets and in oriental food stores.*

SPECIAL OCCASIONS

CHAPTER

13

Admittedly, some foods aren't meant for singles or twosomes. Roast turkey, baked ham, and leg of lamb are best left to larger households where the food will be consumed before it becomes tiresome or spoils.

But don't give up the idea of ever having a festive, even extravagant meal. Instead, choose something designed for one or two.

During Christmas make a Skewered Rib Roast from a single beef rib and serve it with its classic accompaniment, Yorkshire Pudding. Serve the refreshing Walnut, Endive, and Gorgonzola Salad after the entree to cleanse the palate. Highlight the meat with a Cabernet Sauvignon from the Alexander Valley (the 1981s are recommended) in California's Sonoma district.

Rock Cornish Hens with Fruited Cornbread Stuffing are wonderful for Thanksgiving. Bake an acorn squash and flavor it with cinnamon and brown sugar (follow the basic directions for butternut squash on page 38) for the vegetable course. For an Eastern dinner, match the hens with Baby Artichokes with Capers and Shrimp instead of squash.

A Napa Valley Chardonnay, such as the 1982 from Burgess Cellars complements the hens.

Although a four- or five-pound duck may seem a bit large, once it is cooked it provides just enough meat for two servings. Spicy Apricot Chutney is an excellent condiment for the duck; it is sharper tasting than the usual fruit sauces are.

During the spring prepare an appetizer of Asparagus with Blood-Orange Butter Sauce. Blood oranges turn the classic beurre blanc vivid pink. The contrast of green asparagus in a pool of pink sauce is very attractive.

The Alsatian Riesling from Trimbach is a fine accompaniment for the duck; it is much drier than many American made ones.

When soft-shell crabs are in season—May through the summer—make that the meal. Start with a refreshing, delicately tart Tomato Sorbet in place of the salad course. Soft-Shelled Crabs with Tarragon-Hollandaise Sauce are easier to cook for one or two than for twenty. A Sauvignon Blanc from Groth Vineyards in Napa Valley is nice to sip with crab.

Good things come cooked in small quantities.

SKEWERED RIB ROAST

INGREDIENTS

1 rib of a standing rib roast
  (about 2 pounds)
1 clove garlic, peeled
Dash of salt
1 tablespoon vegetable oil
Yorkshire Pudding (follows)

1 Preheat oven to 500 degrees.

2 Bring roast to room temperature. Mash garlic, blending in with a little salt to create a pulp. Mix with the vegetable oil. Rub meat on both sides with the garlic mixture.

3 Place a cooling rack on a jelly-roll pan. Stand the roast on the rack, rib bone up. Insert 2 skewers or other oven-proof, long, sharp, thin pointed objects into the meat. Stick each skewer through fat, not meat, angling downward through the fat and an opening in the rack toward the bottom of the cookie sheet. Cross the first skewer with the second. The effect is a cross that anchors the meat upright.

4 Roast the meat for 15 minutes.

5 Reduce oven temperature to 350 degrees. For medium-rare meat, roast an additional 15 minutes. Add 5 more minutes (a total of 20 minutes at 350 degrees) for medium.

6 Remove the meat from the oven. Pour 2 tablespoons of meat drippings into a 1-quart oven-proof casserole, increase oven temperature to 450 degrees and place the casserole in the oven. Cover the meat loosely with foil to keep warm.

7 Prepare Yorkshire Pudding. About 5 minutes before it is done, start carving the meat. Free the meat from the bone and either slice it into 2 steaks or into long thin slices.

PHOTO OPPOSITE PAGE 132

YORKSHIRE PUDDING

INGREDIENTS

2 tablespoons beef drippings
½ cup all-purpose flour
Dash of salt
½ cup milk
1 egg
1 tablespoon fresh, chopped
  parsley

1 Preheat oven to 450 degrees.

2 Pour drippings into 1-quart oven-proof casserole. Place casserole in oven to keep warm while mixing batter.

3 Stir together flour and salt in a blender or electric mixer. Beat in milk and egg to make a smooth batter. Stir in the parsley. Spoon batter into prepared dish. Bake, uncovered for 15 to 20 minutes, or until the pudding is puffed and brown. Cut the pudding into 4 wedges; 2 per serving.

PHOTO OPPOSITE PAGE 132

WALNUT, ENDIVE, AND GORGONZOLA SALAD

INGREDIENTS

3½ tablespoons walnut oil,
    divided
1 tablespoon chopped
    walnuts
2 teaspoons lemon juice
Salt and freshly ground white
    pepper to taste
2 small heads (2 to 3 inches
    long) Belgian endive

1 cup torn lettuce (Bibb or
    Boston), washed and dried
4 tablespoons crumbled
    Gorgonzola cheese

1 In a small skillet, heat 1 tablespoon walnut oil. Add walnuts and sauté 2 to 3 minutes until lightly browned. Remove from heat. Whisk together remaining 2½ tablespoons oil and lemon juice. Add walnuts and any oil left in the skillet. Season with salt and white pepper.

2 Separate endive into leaves. Wash and dry. Arrange in a salad bowl with lettuce. Sprinkle on cheese. Just before serving, pour on all or part of dressing and toss gently, but well. Serve immediately.

NOTE *Recipe can be halved.*

ROCK CORNISH HENS WITH FRUITED CORNBREAD STUFFING

INGREDIENTS

¼ cup golden raisins
1 tablespoon brandy
2 Rock Cornish hens, thawed
*   if frozen*
1 small lemon
4 tablespoons butter, divided
½ cup minced onion
½ cup diced tart apple,
*   unpeeled*
1 tablespoon fresh, minced
*   parsley*

1 cup cornbread crumbs (see
*   note)*
1 teaspoon fresh minced
*   thyme or ⅓ to ½ teaspoon*
*   dried, crushed thyme*
Salt and freshly ground white
*   pepper to taste*
2 bacon strips, halved
¼ cup Riesling or similar
*   white wine*

1 Combine raisins and brandy in a cup. Stir and set aside 1 hour.

2 Preheat oven to 350 degrees.

3 Rinse hens inside and out with water and pat dry. Grate ½ teaspoon rind from lemon and set aside. Cut lemon in half and rub insides and outsides of hens with cut side of lemon. Set hens aside. Discard lemon halves.

4 Melt 3 tablespoons of butter in a medium skillet. Add onion and sauté over very low heat for 10 minutes, until onion just begins to turn brown. Remove from heat.

5 In a bowl, combine apple, parsley, cornbread crumbs, thyme, reserved lemon rind, raisins, and any brandy left in the cup. Stir. Add onions and butter remaining in the skillet. Stir well. Season with salt and white pepper.

6 Divide mixture between the two hens. There's no need to truss the birds. Place the hens in a shallow roasting pan just large enough to hold them. (A 9- or 10-inch ceramic quiche dish is suitable.) Arrange 2 bacon strips over each breast in a cross.

Dot each bird with ½ tablespoon remaining butter. Pour the wine into the dish.

7 Bake for 60 to 75 minutes. Baste every 15 minutes with pan juices. Halfway through cooking time, turn birds around, so the sides that were touching are now facing outside. Remove to serving plates and serve immediately.

PHOTO OPPOSITE PAGE 117

NOTE *A cup of cornbread crumbs is about 1 large muffin with crusty parts removed. This recipe can be halved.*

BABY ARTICHOKES WITH CAPERS AND SHRIMP

INGREDIENTS

4 small artichokes (each
  about 1½ inches in
  diameter)
1 tablespoon vegetable oil
1 teaspoon salt
2 to 3 tablespoons olive oil
1 large clove garlic, peeled
  and smashed
1 tablespoon capers

½ cup cooked baby shrimp
  or cooked, coarsely
  chopped full-size shrimp

1 Place artichokes in medium pot with vegetable oil, salt and just enough boiling water to cover. Cover pot. Reduce heat to low boil and cook about 20 minutes, or until leaf pulled off is tender.

2 Meanwhile, heat olive oil with garlic, in large skillet, stirring occasionally so garlic permeates oil, about 5 minutes. Add capers and shrimp to warm through. Remove artichokes from water and add to oil. Toss to coat. Spoon artichokes, capers, oil, and shrimp onto 2 plates. Discard garlic. Serve hot or tepid.

PHOTO OPPOSITE PAGE 20

NOTE *This dish can also be made using medium or large artichokes. Quarter 1 artichoke. Cook for 20 minutes, as directed above, until the leaves are tender. Cut out the choke in the center, then add the artichoke quarters to the oil and shrimp combination.*

For a luncheon entree, use 2 medium or large artichokes and double the olive oil, garlic, capers, and shrimp.

ROAST DUCK WITH APRICOT CHUTNEY

INGREDIENTS

1 small navel orange
1 duck (about 4 pounds)
Salt and freshly ground black
   pepper to taste
1½ cups dried apricot halves,
   cut into slivers
1 tablespoon minced
   gingerroot
1 small clove garlic, minced
1 scallion, green and white
   parts, minced

½ teaspoon red pepper flakes
½ teaspoon mustard seed
1 teaspoon tamarind paste
   (see note)
½ cup brown sugar
½ cup cider vinegar
1 to 2 tablespoons water
   (optional)
Bunch of watercress for
   garnish

1 Preheat oven to 450 degrees.

2 Cut orange in half horizontally. Carefully scoop flesh out of orange, leaving shell halves intact. Set orange shells aside. These will be used as cups for the chutney.

3 Rinse duck inside and out with water. Pat dry. Season cavity with salt and pepper. Place orange flesh in duck cavity. Place duck on a rack in a shallow roasting pan. Pierce duck in fatty areas with a small, sharp knife. Place in oven.

4 Meanwhile, prepare chutney: Combine apricot pieces, gingerroot, garlic, scallion, red pepper flakes, mustard seed, tamarind paste, brown sugar, and vinegar in a small heavy-bottomed pot. Cover and cook over very low heat 45 minutes to 1 hour, until thickened and syrupy. If mixture is pasty, rather than the consistency of jam or conserves, add a little water. Season with salt.

5 While chutney is cooking, check duck occasionally. Turn pan around in oven once so duck browns evenly. If necessary, spoon off accumulating fat. Roast duck for 1 hour, or until it is golden brown and tests done.

6 To serve, remove duck from oven. Cut in half lengthwise and place on serving plates. Spoon chutney into the 2 orange halves and place one orange half on each plate. Garnish with watercress. Serve immediately.

PHOTO 2 FOLLOWING PAGE 132

NOTE *Tamarind paste is available two ways: packaged and as part of the tamarind pod. To obtain flesh from the pod, peel off the flaky brown skin and scrape out the chewy, sticky brown paste. Tamarind paste and pods are available in Caribbean and Hispanic food stores. You can substitute 1 teaspoon grated lemon rind for the tart-tasting tamarind.*

OPPOSITE: Skewered Rib Roast (page 125) with Yorkshire Pudding (page 126).

FOLLOWING PHOTO: Roast Duck with Apricot Chutney (page 131).

ASPARAGUS WITH BLOOD-ORANGE BUTTER SAUCE

INGREDIENTS

*½ pound fresh asparagus,
washed and tough ends
snapped off
2 tablespoons minced shallots
2 tablespoons juice from
blood oranges (see note)
¼ cup dry white wine*

*½ cup butter, cold, cut in
½-inch slices
Salt and freshly ground white
pepper to taste*

1 Bring a large skillet with water to the boil. Add asparagus in a single layer and cook at a low boil until fork tender, 8 to 15 minutes, depending on the thickness of the spears. Remove and drain well. Keep hot while preparing butter sauce.

2 Combine shallots, orange juice, and white wine in a small pot. Bring to a boil and cook over high heat until the mixture is reduced to 2 tablespoons.

3 Turn off heat. Add 1 piece of butter and whisk in until blended. Then add another piece of butter. Continue the process, working fast and adding more butter as soon as the previous chunk has dissolved into the mixture. About halfway through, the pot may become so cool that the butter doesn't melt in. If so, turn on heat to very low temperature and add more butter. The butter should melt into a creamy mixture, not liquify. Season with salt and white pepper.

4 Pour butter sauce onto a serving platter. Top with asparagus spears. Serve immediately.

NOTE *If blood oranges aren't available, use any mild-flavored juice orange.*

OPPOSITE: Asparagus with Blood-Orange
Butter Sauce.

PRECEDING PHOTO: Baked Apples with
Crème Anglaise (page 139).

SOFT-SHELLED CRABS WITH TARRAGON SAUCE

INGREDIENTS

6 soft-shelled crabs, cleaned
Tarragon Sauce (page 135)
4 tablespoons all-purpose
  flour
1/4 teaspoon salt
Dash of freshly ground black
  pepper

1/2 to 3/4 teaspoon fresh,
  minced or 1/4 teaspoon
  dried tarragon, crushed
1/4 cup butter

1 Wash crabs and pat completely dry. Prepare Tarragon Sauce and set over hot water in top of double boiler to keep warm.

2 Combine flour, salt, pepper, and tarragon. Dust crabs on both sides in flour mixture. Set aside for a minute. Meanwhile, melt butter in large skillet over medium heat until bubbly. Add crabs (don't crowd; cook only half at a time, if necessary) and sauté 3 to 4 minutes on one side. Turn over and cook on second side 2 to 3 minutes, or until nicely browned. Remove to a warm plate and cook remaining crabs.

3 Place crabs on 2 serving plates and spoon Tarragon Sauce over. Serve immediately.

PHOTO 3 FOLLOWING PAGE 20

NOTE *Recipe can be halved.*

TARRAGON SAUCE

INGREDIENTS

2 egg yolks, at room
  temperature
1/2 cup butter, melted
1/2 tablespoon shallot-flavored
  vinegar
1/4 teaspoon salt
1/2 to 3/4 teaspoon fresh,
  minced or 1/4 teaspoon
  dried tarragon, crushed
Dash of freshly ground white
  pepper

1 Place egg yolks in blender or food processor container fitted with a steel blade. Very slowly trickle in melted butter.

2 When mixture thickens and all the butter is added, turn machine off and add vinegar, salt, tarragon, and white pepper. Stir by hand.

PHOTO 3 FOLLOWING PAGE 20. MAKES ABOUT 1/2 CUP SAUCE

NOTE *Recipe can be halved.*

TOMATO SORBET

INGREDIENTS

1 cup peeled, seeded tomato pieces (about 2 medium tomatoes)
1 tablespoon fresh, minced dill
1½ tablespoons tomato paste
1 tablespoon lemon juice
1½ teaspoons grated lemon rind

1½ tablespoons sugar syrup (see note)
Dill sprigs for garnish

1 In blender or food processor, combine tomato pieces, dill, tomato paste, lemon juice, lemon rind, and sugar syrup. Process to a pulp. Mixture may be chunky rather than smooth, but that's fine.

2 Either pour into an ice cream maker and process according to manufacturer's directions, or pour into an ice cube tray and freeze until slushy, stirring occasionally to break up ice chunks (about 2 hours).

3 Spoon sorbet into 2 saucer champagne cups and garnish with dill sprigs. Serve immediately.

NOTE *To make sugar syrup combine 2 tablespoons water with 2 tablespoons sugar in a small saucepan. Bring to a boil, reduce heat and cook until sugar dissolves. Cool.*

DESSERTS

CHAPTER

14

Like everything else, preferences in desserts depend on the season and the preceding meal.

For example, during the summer when plums are at their tart and juicy best make a feast of them in a Plum Cobbler. Serve this homey, fruity dish after a light dinner, such as Scallop Salad and Eggplant Steaks.

To erase the memory of garlic-laden Linguini with Mussels Sauce, prepare frothy Zabaglione. It's marvelous over fresh raspberries, strawberries, or blackberries.

During the winter, turn to Frosted Chocolate Brownie Cake, good with a cup of coffee or a glass of milk. A stack of Butter Cookies and a cup of hot chocolate are the perfect combination for whiling away a chilly Sunday afternoon.

While all the recipes in this chapter are scaled down, some yield more than one or two servings. Surely you'll be able to use up these luscious leftovers.

PLUM COBBLER

INGREDIENTS

3 large plums
5 tablespoons sugar, divided
¼ teaspoon ground
  cinnamon
½ cup all-purpose flour
¾ teaspoon baking powder
Dash of salt
1 tablespoon butter
2 to 3 tablespoons heavy
  cream

1 Preheat oven to 400 degrees.

2 Wash fruit and pat dry. Pit and slice plums into thin, lengthwise slices to yield 2½ to 3 cups.

3 Spoon fruit into a 1-quart oven-proof casserole. Combine 4 tablespoons sugar with cinnamon. Sprinkle over the plums. Bake for 10 minutes. Meanwhile, prepare topping.

4 Combine flour, remaining 1 tablespoon sugar, baking powder, and salt. Stir well. Cut butter into slivers and use pastry blender to cut butter into flour mixture, until flour is crumbly. Add cream, 1 tablespoon at a time, stirring with a fork, until the dough comes together.

5 Turn out onto a floured board. Flour a rolling pin and roll dough ½-inch thick. Use cookie cutters to cut out desired shapes. Remove the cobbler from the oven. Arrange the dough over the fruit. (It may be necessary to smooth out the fruit.)

6 Return the cobbler to the oven (400 degrees) and bake an additional 15 to 20 minutes, until the dough browns lightly. Serve hot or tepid.

BAKED APPLES WITH CRÈME ANGLAISE

INGREDIENTS

2 tablespoons raisins
2 tablespoons dark rum or
  brandy
1 cup half-and-half
2 egg yolks
¼ cup sugar

Dash of salt
1 teaspoon vanilla
2 medium Rome Beauty or
  Cortland apples
1 tablespoon butter

1 Soak raisins in rum or brandy for at least 1 hour.

2 Heat half-and-half in small heavy-bottomed pot until very hot. Do not allow to come to a boil.

3 Meanwhile, in top of double boiler, whisk together egg yolks, sugar, and salt. Place over water held at a simmer in the bottom of a double boiler. Slowly pour in half-and-half, stirring constantly. Continue to stir, keeping top of double boiler over simmering water until the mixture thickens to the consistency of pancake batter. Don't rush it, or the sauce may curdle.

4 When done, remove from heat and allow sauce to cool to room temperature. Add vanilla. Cover with plastic wrap and chill.

5 Preheat oven to 375 degrees.

6 When ready to bake apples, core each, halfway down, but do not puncture through the bottom. Peel off about ⅓ of the skin around the top. Spoon raisins with the liquor into the apple cavities. Top each apple with half the butter.

7 Place the apples in a 1-quart oven-proof casserole and bake for 30 minutes, basting once or twice with pan juices. Apples are done when they can be easily pierced with a knife tip.

8 To serve, place each apple in a bowl. Pour chilled sauce over each. Apples should be hot; sauce cold for a refreshing match.

PHOTO 3 FOLLOWING PAGE 132

EGGNOG CUSTARD

INGREDIENTS

2 eggs
1 egg yolk
2 tablespoons sugar
½ teaspoon vanilla
2 tablespoons dark rum
¾ cup half-and-half
Ground nutmeg
Rum Syrup (recipe follows)

1 Preheat oven to 325 degrees.

2 Whisk together eggs, egg yolk, sugar, vanilla, rum, and half-and-half. Pour into greased 2-cup oven-proof casserole.

3 Place casserole in larger cake pan. Pour enough hot water into second pan to come halfway up sides of casserole. Sprinkle custard lightly with ground nutmeg. Bake for 45 minutes, or until knife inserted near the center comes out clean. Spoon half of Rum Syrup into each of 2 bowls. Top with the Eggnog Custard.

RUM SYRUP

INGREDIENTS

¼ cup sugar
¼ cup water
1½ to 2 tablespoons dark
  rum

1 Combine sugar and water in a small pot. Bring to a boil. Reduce heat to medium and allow the mixture to cook at a low boil for 5 to 10 minutes, until it is syrupy.

2 Remove from heat. Cool until just warm. Add rum.

POACHED PEARS

INGREDIENTS

½ cup sugar
½ cup water
¾ cup Chenin Blanc or
  similar white wine
¼ cup dry Sherry
1 cinnamon stick
3 to 4 whole cloves
¼ teaspoon ground ginger
2 ripe pears, cored, halved,
  and peeled

1 Combine sugar, water, wine, Sherry, cinnamon, cloves, and ginger in medium pot. Bring to a boil. Reduce heat and simmer 5 minutes.

2 Meanwhile, prepare pears. Add pears to saucepan and simmer 20 minutes, until fork tender. Remove pears from syrup. Bring syrup to a boil again and boil about 5 to 8 minutes, or until syrup is reduced by half and slightly thickened. Pour syrup over pears in a serving dish and add cinnamon stick. Chill for 1 to 2 hours. Remove cinnamon stick. Serve pears with syrup.

NOTE *The above recipe provides the basic technique for poaching fruit. You can use it for poaching apples or plums as well.*

Poached fruit will keep in the refrigerator, covered with the poaching syrup, for several days. The fruit and syrup are a nice addition to a slice of angel food cake or pound cake.

The recipe can be halved; use 1 cinnamon stick however.

BANANAS IN RUM SAUCE

INGREDIENTS

1 medium banana (firm, but
   ripe)
1 tablespoon butter
1 teaspoon mild-flavored
   vegetable oil
1 tablespoon apricot jam
1/16 teaspoon ground nutmeg
1 tablespoon dark rum
1 scoop vanilla ice cream

1 Slice banana lengthwise in half, then crosswise in half to form 4 quarters. Melt butter in small skillet with oil. Add banana slices and sauté over medium heat, shaking pan continually for 3 to 5 minutes. Add jam and stir. Add nutmeg and stir again.

2 Remove from heat. Immediately pour in rum and light with a match. Turn pan to send rum flames around banana slices. When flame dies naturally, pour banana slices with pan liquids over ice cream in a bowl. Serve warm.

SERVES 1

STRAWBERRIES IN GRAND MARNIER

INGREDIENTS

½ cup sliced strawberries
1 tablespoon Grand Marnier
  or other orange-flavored
  liqueur
¼ teaspoon grated lemon
  rind
Confectioners' sugar

1 Combine strawberries, Grand Marnier, and lemon rind in small serving bowl.

2 Add a light dusting of confectioners' sugar—about a teaspoonful—and toss berries gently.

3 Set aside for 15 to 30 minutes for flavors to blend.

SERVES 1

BLUEBERRY MOUSSE

INGREDIENTS

1 teaspoon unflavored gelatin
1/4 cup sugar
2/3 cup pureed blueberries
 (about 1 1/3 cups
 blueberries)
1 egg yolk
Lemon juice
1/4 teaspoon almond extract
1/2 cup heavy cream, whipped

1 Mix gelatin, sugar, and blueberry puree in top of double boiler. Set over simmering water and heat. Stir frequently until sugar and gelatin dissolve.

2 Beat the egg yolk. Stir a little of the hot blueberry mixture into the yolk, then stir all the yolk mixture into the blueberries. Cook over low heat, stirring constantly until the mixture is slightly thickened.

3 Taste the mixture and if it doesn't have a slightly tart flavor add a few drops of lemon juice. The amount will vary each time according to the berries. Don't overdo it however. Stir in the almond extract.

4 Remove from heat. Cool to room temperature, then chill until mixture thickens, about 1 hour. Whip cream until stiff. Fold into blueberry mixture. Spoon into 2 serving cups. Chill about 2 hours.

NOTE *If desired, substitute raspberries for the blueberries and omit the lemon juice.*

ZABAGLIONE

INGREDIENTS

*2 egg yolks, at room
    temperature
3 tablespoons sugar
2 tablespoons Marsala wine
1½ cups fresh sliced
    strawberries, raspberries,
    or peaches*

1 Place egg yolks, sugar, and Marsala in top of double boiler over simmering water. Beat constantly with a whisk until the mixture is light and frothy, about 5 to 10 minutes.

2 Divide fruit between 2 bowls and spoon zabaglione over. Serve immediately.

NOTE *This dish is deceptively simple, but requires that you follow directions exactly. If the mixture becomes too hot you'll have cooked egg yolks rather than a frothy mass, and if you don't beat the mixture long enough it will be thin and unappealing.*

    The air beaten into the combination of egg yolks, sugar, and Marsala wine vanishes quickly. Have the fruit prepared and in serving bowls. Pour on the zabaglione once it is the consistency of half-whipped cream and serve.

CARAMEL PUFFERY

INGREDIENTS

¼ cup water
2 tablespoons butter, cut in
*   chunks*
¼ cup cake flour
Dash of salt
1 egg, at room temperature
2 scoops vanilla ice cream
Caramel Sauce (recipe
*   follows)*

1 Preheat oven to 375 degrees.

2 Combine water and butter in a small pot. Bring to a boil. Stir in cake flour and salt, all at once. Reduce heat to very low. Stir constantly until dough comes together into a smooth ball. Remove from heat. Cool 5 minutes. Beat in egg.

3 Drop mixture from heaping tablespoonfuls onto greased and floured cookie sheet to form 2 balls. Bake for 30 to 35 minutes, or until golden brown. Turn off heat. Remove puffs. Slice puffs horizontally. Pull out any wet dough and discard. Return puffs to oven for 15 to 20 minutes to dry.

4 Place bottom of one puff on each of 2 serving plates. Place a scoop of ice cream into each bottom and cover with top half of each puff. Spoon warm Caramel Sauce over puffs and serve immediately.

PHOTO 2 FOLLOWING PAGE 148

CARAMEL SAUCE

INGREDIENTS

*¹/₂ cup plus 2 tablespoons
  sugar*
¹/₄ cup butter
¹/₂ cup heavy cream
Dash of salt

1 Place sugar in small, heavy-bottomed pot. Place over very low heat and allow sugar to liquify, shaking pot frequently. This process should take 20 to 30 minutes.

2 Cut butter into chunks and add to liquified sugar. Mixture will bubble and sputter and will separate. Add cream and salt and stir constantly until smooth. This sauce is very thin. Allow to cool until it is warm and slightly thickened.

3 Either serve warm soon after preparing it, or refrigerate, covered, and reheat in top of a double boiler over simmering water.

MAKES ABOUT 1 CUP SAUCE

NOTE *This is a lovely sauce over ice cream, bananas, pound cake, or even straight by the spoonful.*

RHUBARB CRISP

INGREDIENTS

2 cups sliced rhubarb
¼ cup granulated sugar
2 tablespoons butter
¼ cup all-purpose flour
½ teaspoon ground
  cinnamon
3 tablespoons brown sugar
Vanilla ice cream (optional)

1 Preheat oven to 350 degrees.

2 Combine rhubarb and granulated sugar. Toss well and spoon into an ovenproof 1-quart casserole. Cut butter into slivers. Combine flour and cinnamon in a small bowl. Cut in butter until mixture resembles coarse crumbs. Add brown sugar and toss.

3 Sprinkle this mixture over the rhubarb. Bake for 30 minutes or until topping is browned and fruit is slightly bubbly. Divide rhubarb mixture between two dessert bowls. If desired, top with ice cream.

NOTE *Other fruit such as strawberries, fresh peaches, nectarines, or plums can be used in place of rhubarb. It may be necessary to reduce the sugar to 2 tablespoons if using one of these sweeter fruits.*

OPPOSITE: Rhubarb Crisp.
FOLLOWING PHOTO: Caramel Puffery (page 146).

STRAWBERRY-RHUBARB CLAFOUTI

INGREDIENTS

1 cup each sliced strawberries
 and sliced rhubarb
¹⁄₄ cup plus 1 tablespoon
 sugar
³⁄₄ cup half-and-half or milk
1 egg
3 tablespoons flour
¹⁄₄ teaspoon ground nutmeg

1 Preheat oven to 375 degrees.

2 Place strawberries and rhubarb in a 1-quart ovenproof casserole. Sprinkle with 1 tablespoon sugar and bake 10 minutes. Remove and set aside while making batter.

3 Whisk together ¹⁄₄ cup sugar, half-and-half or milk, and egg. Stir in flour and nutmeg and stir to remove any lumps. Pour batter over fruit. Return to oven for 40 minutes or until mixture is lightly browned and as firm as a shimmering custard. Remove from oven and let stand about 10 minutes until just warm.

NOTE *This does not taste as good cold. Either prepare the dish just before serving, or reheat.*

OPPOSITE: Pecan-Maple Pie (page 150).

PRECEDING PHOTO: Frosted Chocolate Brownie Cake (page 152) with Chocolate Cream Cheese Frosting (page 153).

PECAN-MAPLE PIE

INGREDIENTS

1 Small Pie Crust (recipe
follows)
1 egg, lightly beaten
¼ cup light corn syrup
2 tablespoons maple syrup
2 tablespoons brown sugar
Dash of salt
2 tablespoons butter, melted
⅔ cup pecan halves

1 Preheat oven to 425 degrees. Partially bake pie crust 5 minutes. Set aside to cool.

2 Reduce oven temperature to 350 degrees.

3 Stir together egg, corn syrup, maple syrup, brown sugar, salt, and butter. Stir in pecan halves. Gently pour into pie crust.

4 Place on jelly-roll pan in case pie bubbles over. Bake for 30 minutes. Pie may be a little loose. Allow to cool 30 minutes before removing sides of tart pan and slicing.

PHOTO OPPOSITE PAGE 149. MAKES 2 TO 4 SERVINGS

SMALL PIE CRUST

INGREDIENTS

½ cup all-purpose flour
Dash of salt
2 tablespoons cold butter, cut
  into small pieces
1 tablespoon vegetable
  shortening
1 egg yolk beaten with
  1 tablespoon cold water

1 Mix together flour and salt in a bowl. Cut in butter pieces and vegetable shortening until mixture resembles coarse meal. Pour in egg mixture and stir with a fork until the mixture holds together.

2 Dough should be very soft, but not sticky. Wrap in plastic wrap and refrigerate 30 minutes.

3 Roll out on a floured board, to a 10-inch circle, using a floured rolling pin. Gently ease into 7-inch tart pan with removable bottom.

FROSTED CHOCOLATE BROWNIE CAKE

INGREDIENTS

*1 bar (3 ounces) semisweet
    chocolate
1/2 cup butter
1/2 cup sugar
3/4 teaspoon vanilla
Dash of salt
2 eggs
1/2 cup all-purpose flour
Chocolate Cream Cheese
    Frosting (recipe follows)*

1 Preheat oven to 350 degrees.

2 In top of double boiler, over hot water, break in chocolate bar. Add butter and allow to melt, stirring occasionally. Remove from heat. Add sugar, vanilla, salt, and eggs, and stir well. Add flour and stir until thoroughly mixed.

3 Spread batter in greased and floured 8-inch round cake pan. Bake for 30 to 35 minutes or until cake tests done. Remove from oven. Cool in pan about 30 minutes. Turn out onto wire rack and cool completely.

4 Prepare Chocolate Cream Cheese Frosting.

5 Slice cake in half to form 2 half circles. Spread top of one half with some of frosting. Cover with remaining half of cake. Frost top and sides of cake with remaining frosting.

PHOTO 3 FOLLOWING PAGE 148. SERVES 2 TO 4

CHOCOLATE CREAM CHEESE FROSTING

INGREDIENTS

*1 bar (3 ounces) semisweet
 chocolate*
1 teaspoon vegetable oil
3 ounces cream cheese
½ teaspoon vanilla
1 cup confectioners' sugar
1 to 3 teaspoons heavy cream

1 Melt together chocolate and oil in top of double boiler over boiling water.

2 Meanwhile, beat cream cheese until light. Add vanilla and chocolate mixture and beat again. Gradually stir in confectioners' sugar. Add cream by the teaspoon to reach a light and spreadable frosting consistency.

PHOTO 3 FOLLOWING PAGE 148

CARROT CUPCAKES

INGREDIENTS

½ cup all-purpose flour
½ cup sugar
1 teaspoon ground cinnamon
½ teaspoon baking soda
Dash of salt
3 ounces (⅓ cup plus 1
   tablespoon) vegetable oil
1 egg, beaten

1½ teaspoons vanilla
¾ cup grated carrots
Frosting (recipe follows)

1 Preheat oven to 350 degrees.

2 Combine flour, sugar, cinnamon, baking soda, and salt in a bowl and stir to combine well. Stir together oil, egg, and vanilla, and pour into flour mixture. Beat briefly by hand or in electric mixer. Add carrots and stir well.

3 Grease 6 muffin cups and pour in batter to come ⅔ the way up the cups. If batter almost fills cups, make a 7th cupcake. Bake for 25 to 30 minutes. Cool cupcakes in pan about 30 minutes, then carefully work a knife around the edges of the cupcakes and gently remove each one to cool thoroughly.

4 Prepare Frosting. When cupcakes have cooled, spread each top generously with frosting. Either serve immediately or refrigerate. If refrigerating more than a few hours, chill first to firm up frosting, then loosely wrap cupcakes with plastic wrap.

MAKES 6 GENEROUSLY FROSTED CUPCAKES OR 7 ADEQUATELY FROSTED ONES

FROSTING

INGREDIENTS

3 ounces cream cheese
2 tablespoons unsalted butter
¼ teaspoon vanilla
6 tablespoons confectioners'
  sugar

1 Cream together cheese, butter, and vanilla until light.

2 Gradually beat in confectioners' sugar.

QUARTER POUNDER CAKE

INGREDIENTS

¹/₂ cup butter
³/₄ cup sugar
2 eggs, at room temperature
1 cup cake flour
¹/₄ teaspoon salt
¹/₄ teaspoon ground nutmeg
¹/₃ cup chopped black walnuts
  or pecans

1 Preheat oven to 325 degrees.

2 Cream butter until light. Slowly add sugar, beating well to make a creamy mixture. Add eggs, one at a time, beating well after each addition. Stir in flour, salt, and nutmeg. Combine well. Fold in nuts.

3 Spoon batter into greased and floured 7½-by-3½-inch loaf pan. Bake for 1 hour, or until cake tests done with a toothpick. Cool in pan for 10 minutes, turn out onto cooling rack and finish cooling before slicing.

MAKES 1 LOAF; ABOUT 6 SLICES

NOTE *This is an attractive loaf for gift giving, especially if you know a single who doesn't like to have large quantities of sweets around the house.*
  Wrap the loaf in plastic wrap and include a small loaf pan and the recipe as part of the gift.

BUTTER COOKIES

INGREDIENTS

*¹/₂ cup butter, at room
    temperature*
*6 tablespoons confectioners'
    sugar*
Dash of salt
¹/₂ teaspoon vanilla
1 cup sifted flour
*6 tablespoons chopped
    pecans*

1 Preheat oven to 350 degrees.

2 In electric mixer bowl (or by hand), combine butter, confectioners' sugar, salt, and vanilla. Blend on low speed until creamy. Gradually add flour, about ¼ cup at a time, beating in before adding more. Stir in chopped pecans.

3 Measure out dough by level tablespoon. Roll into balls and place 2 inches apart on ungreased cookie sheet. Flatten to ½-inch thickness using fork tines. Bake for 20 minutes, or until cookies are lightly browned. Allow to cool on cookie sheet 10 minutes, then remove to rack to cool completely.

MAKES 18 COOKIES

NOTE *I adore these cookies.*
    They are so rich and buttery, yet not too sweet to be indulged in. Once you become hooked on these (and I'm sure you will) prepare a double or triple batch.
    Place any extras in a plastic container and freeze.
    The dough also freezes well. I'd suggest making the cookie shapes and freezing them. Arrange the frozen cookies on a cookie sheet and add about 5 to 10 minutes on to the baking time.

LIME BARS

INGREDIENTS

¹/₂ cup butter
1 cup all-purpose flour
¹/₄ cup confectioners' sugar
2 eggs
1 cup granulated sugar
6 tablespoons fresh lime juice
  plus 1 tablespoon lime pulp
1 tablespoon cornstarch
1 teaspoon grated lime rind

1 Preheat oven to 350 degrees.

2 Cut butter in small pieces. Place flour and confectioners' sugar in a bowl. Cut in butter until mixture is coarse grained. Pat firmly into a 9-inch square pan. Bake for 10 minutes. Set aside to cool while making filling.

3 In a small bowl, combine eggs and granulated sugar. Stir together lime juice, pulp, and cornstarch, mixing well so no lumps remain. Stir lime-juice mixture into egg combination. Stir in lime rind. Pour over baked crust. Return to oven and bake 30 to 40 minutes longer. Cool, then cut into squares to serve.

MAKES 16 BARS

NOTE *You can, of course, use lemon juice and pulp in place of lime juice. I prefer the lime since it has a sharper flavor. You could also try orange juice, but add a tablespoon of grated orange rind instead of the teaspoon.*

   These bars freeze well. Wrap them individually, so you'll have as little as you need.

MOCHA BROWNIES

INGREDIENTS

4 ounces (4 squares)
  unsweetened chocolate
1 cup butter
¼ cup instant coffee powder
2 cups sugar
3 eggs, beaten
½ teaspoon vanilla
1 cup all-purpose flour
¼ teaspoon salt

1 Preheat oven to 350 degrees.

2 Combine chocolate, butter, and coffee powder in top of a double boiler over simmering water. Melt mixture, stirring occasionally. Remove from heat.

3 Add sugar, stirring well. Then add eggs and vanilla. Stir together flour and salt. Add to batter. Pour into greased and floured 9-inch square pan. Bake for 45 minutes. Top of brownies will be glossy, but the inside should be moist and fudgy.

MAKES 20 BROWNIES

NOTE *Do not cut until thoroughly chilled. These brownies keep very well in the refrigerator, and even better in the freezer where they will be beyond temptation.*

CHOCOLATE COOKIES

INGREDIENTS

¼ cup butter, at room
  temperature
3 tablespoons confectioners'
  sugar
Dash of salt
4 tablespoons all-purpose
  flour
3 tablespoons good-quality
  unsweetened cocoa

1 Preheat oven to 350 degrees.

2 In electric mixer bowl (or by hand), combine butter, confectioners' sugar, and salt. Blend on low speed until creamy. Gradually add flour a tablespoon at a time. When blended, add cocoa, a tablespoon at a time. Don't overbeat or mixture will become oily.

3 Working quickly, measure out dough by level table-spoonfuls. Roll into balls and place 2 inches apart on ungreased cookie sheet. Flatten with fork tines to ½-inch thickness. Bake for 15 minutes. Allow to cool on cookie sheet for 10 minutes, then remove to cooling rack to cool completely.

MAKES 7 OR 8 COOKIES

PIG-OUT CHOCOLATE CHIP COOKIES

INGREDIENTS

¼ cup butter
2 tablespoons granulated
  sugar
¼ cup firmly packed brown
  sugar
2 tablespoons beaten egg
½ teaspoon vanilla extract
¹⁄₁₆ teaspoon almond extract
½ cup all-purpose flour

¼ teaspoon baking soda
Dash of salt
1 bar (3 ounces) semisweet
  chocolate, broken into
  small bits

1 Preheat oven to 350 degrees.

2 Cream butter, granulated sugar, and brown sugar until light. Add egg, vanilla, and almond extracts and mix well. Stir together flour, baking soda, and salt. Gradually add to butter mixture, stirring well. Fold in chocolate pieces.

3 Spoon batter on ungreased cookie sheet, forming 2 circles, about 4½ inches in diameter and ½ inch thick. The cookies will spread to almost double the diameter during baking, so arrange dough accordingly.

4 Bake for 15 minutes. Allow to cool for a few minutes. Then ease cookies with a spatula to loosen but leave on cookie sheet until lukewarm. Remove to a cooling rack to cool completely. Cookies will become firm and chewy.

MAKES 2 MONSTER COOKIES

CHEWY GINGER COOKIES

INGREDIENTS

6 tablespoons butter
1/2 cup sugar
1 egg, beaten
1 tablespoon maple syrup
1 tablespoon dark molasses
1 cup all-purpose flour
1 teaspoon baking soda
Dash of salt
2 teaspoons ground ginger

1/2 teaspoon ground
  cinnamon
1/4 teaspoon ground nutmeg

1 Preheat oven to 350 degrees.

2 Cream together butter and sugar. Add egg, maple syrup, and molasses and stir well. Sift together flour, baking soda, salt, ginger, cinnamon, and nutmeg. Add to butter mixture and stir well.

3 Drop cookies by rounded tablespoons onto greased and floured cookie sheet, allowing about 1½ inches between cookies.

4 Bake for 12 to 15 minutes, or until cookies begin to brown around the edges. Allow to cool 10 minutes, then remove to cooling rack to cool completely.

MAKES ABOUT 20 COOKIES

NECTARINE SHORTCAKE

INGREDIENTS

½ cup all-purpose flour
1 teaspoon baking powder
1 tablespoon confectioners'
* sugar*
2 tablespoons butter, cut in
* small chunks*
2 to 3 tablespoons milk
2 large nectarines, halved,
* pitted, and cut into small*
* pieces*

1 tablespoon granulated sugar
2 tablespoons peach or
* apricot liqueur*
¼ cup heavy cream, whipped
* or 2 scoops of vanilla ice*
* cream*

1 Preheat oven to 425 degrees.

2 Combine flour, baking powder, and confectioners' sugar in a small bowl. Cut in butter until mixture is crumbly. Stir in milk by the tablespoon, to form dough that comes together. Don't overmix. Shape into 2 biscuits and place on a greased cookie sheet. Bake for 12 to 15 minutes, until lightly browned.

3 While biscuits are baking, combine nectarine pieces, sugar, and liqueur in a small saucepan. Cook over low heat about 10 to 15 minutes, until the mixture thickens and the nectarines are tender.

4 Remove the biscuits from the oven when they are done. Split each biscuit in half and place bottom halves on 2 serving plates. Spread part of the nectarine mixture on the bottom of each biscuit. Top with remaining biscuit half and remaining nectarine mixture. Finally, add a generous dollop of whipped cream or vanilla ice cream to each. Serve immediately.

APRICOT CHEESECAKE

INGREDIENTS

1 cup diced, glazed or
   glacéed apricots (don't use
   the unsweetened dried
   ones)
1/4 cup apricot liqueur
1/2 cup gingersnap crumbs
1/2 tablespoon butter
1 pound cream cheese, at
   room temperature

3/4 cup sugar
4 eggs, at room temperature
1 teaspoon vanilla extract
1/4 cup heavy cream, at room
   temperature

1 Combine apricot pieces and liqueur in a small bowl and set aside for 1 hour, so liqueur is absorbed. Stir occasionally.

2 Toss together gingersnap crumbs and butter. Pat into bottom and about 1/2 inch up the sides of an 8-inch springform pan. Chill in refrigerator while preparing filling.

3 Preheat oven to 300 degrees.

4 Using electric mixer, or a strong arm, blend together cream cheese and sugar until light, in large bowl. Add eggs, one at a time, blending well before adding the next egg. Stir in vanilla extract and cream.

5 Pour about 3/4 of the cream cheese mixture into the prepared pan. Gently spoon in the apricots and any remaining liqueur. (This will sink to the bottom, flavoring the cream cheese along the way.) Top with remaining cream cheese batter.

6 Place springform pan inside 9-inch cake pan filled with 1/2-inch hot water. Bake for 1 hour and 15 minutes or until cake doesn't quiver when shaken. Turn off heat, open oven door and leave cake in oven to rest for 30 minutes. Remove to cool at room temperature another hour, then refrigerate and chill 3 to 4 hours before serving.

SERVES 8

OPPOSITE: Apricot Cheesecake.

A CHEESECAKE LIKE LITTLE JACK'S

INGREDIENTS

¾ cup raisins
6 ounces dry cottage cheese
1 pound cream cheese
¾ cup plus 1 tablespoon
    sugar
6 eggs, at room temperature

1 cup sour cream
1 cup half-and-half
16 graham crackers
3 to 4 tablespoons butter,
    melted
¼ teaspoon cinnamon

1 Preheat oven to 350 degrees.

2 Place raisins in a small bowl. Add boiling water to cover and set aside for 5 minutes, or until raisins plump up.

3 Cream cottage cheese in the large bowl of an electric mixer until the mixture is smooth and individual curds are blended. Blend in cream cheese until light and fluffy. Add ¾ cup sugar gradually, stirring well. Beat in eggs, one at a time, beating well after each addition. Do this by hand. Stir in sour cream and half-and-half.

4 Crush crackers finely using a blender or food processor. Set aside ½ cup graham cracker crumbs. Combine the remaining crumbs with melted butter, adding as much as necessary (3 to 4 tablespoons) to create a mixture that will hold together. Press into bottom of a 9-inch springform pan. Drain raisins well and sprinkle over graham crackers. Gently and slowly pour in cream-cheese mixture.

5 Bake for 1¼ to 1½ hours. Remove from the oven and allow the cake to cool (it may crack) at room temperature. When cake is lukewarm, remove the sides of the pan. Combine remaining ½ cup graham cracker crumbs with remaining 1 tablespoon sugar and cinnamon. Use to dust the top and sides of the cake.

SERVES 10 TO 12

OPPOSITE: Chocolate Raspberry Truffles (page 166).

CHOCOLATE-RASPBERRY TRUFFLES

INGREDIENTS

1 tablespoon raspberry
  liqueur
2 tablespoons heavy cream
2 teaspoons plus 1 tablespoon
  unsalted butter
3 ounces semisweet chocolate,
  broken into pieces
3 ounces high-quality
  bittersweet chocolate,
  broken into pieces

1 Pour raspberry liqueur into a small, heavy-bottomed saucepan and heat over high heat about 30 seconds or until liqueur is reduced by half. Watch closely. Add cream and bring to a boil. Reduce heat and simmer 30 seconds. Again, watch carefully. Remove from heat. Add 2 teaspoons butter and the semisweet chocolate. Stir with wooden spoon until mixture is smooth and melted. Place saucepan in refrigerator until mixture is solid, 1 to 2 hours.

2 Spoon out chocolate and quickly shape into balls about 1½-inches in diameter. Make a total of 6. Place the balls on a foil-lined plate and freeze for 1 hour.

3 Combine bittersweet chocolate and 1 tablespoon butter in top of double boiler. Place over water heated to 120 degrees. Let mixture sit for 5 minutes, then gently stir with a wooden spoon until mixture is melted and smooth. Remove pan with chocolate and set aside. Pour off some of the hot water and add enough cold water to the bottom of the boiler so the water registers 86 to 90 degrees. Again place the pan with the chocolate over the water and let it cool to 86 to 90 degrees, stirring occasionally.

4 Remove the chocolate centers from the freezer. Place a sheet of foil on a plate. Dip the centers, one at a time in the melted chocolate, turning to coat all sides. Then set on the foil. Repeat until all 6 centers are chocolate covered. There may be leftover melted chocolate in the pan; if so, spoon onto the truffles for a thicker coating. Let the chocolate firm up at room temperature, then refrigerate until serving.

PHOTO OPPOSITE PAGE 165. MAKES 6 TRUFFLES

CARAMEL PEARS

INGREDIENTS

2 ripe pears
¹/₂ pound good-quality
chocolate caramels
1 tablespoon dark rum
¹/₄ cup chopped almonds or
pecans
¹/₄ cup chocolate chips

1 Choose 2 firm, ripe pears with good-sized stems. Wash and dry and set aside.

2 In top of a double boiler, over boiling water, place caramels and rum. Reduce heat to low and allow caramels to melt, stirring occasionally.

3 Meanwhile pour nuts and chocolate chips onto a piece of wax paper and mix together. Set out a second sheet of wax paper for the pears to dry on.

4 When caramel has melted, place one pear in the pan and roll it around in the caramel. Spoon some of the sauce over the pear so it is completely covered.

5 Next set the bottom of the pear in the nut-chocolate combination. Set aside on the second piece of paper and allow to firm up. Repeat the process with the second pear.

6 Either serve when firm, or wrap the pears in plastic wrap and store in the refrigerator up to 3 days.

NOTE *Depending on how you dip the pears, you may have some caramel sauce and nuts left over. If so, stir the nuts into the caramels and drop this mixture by teaspoonfuls onto wax paper and allow to harden. Serve as candy.*
Recipe can be halved.

CRACKLING BANANAS

INGREDIENTS

1 cup sugar
¼ cup honey
¼ cup water
1 very large or 2 small ripe,
  green-tipped bananas

1 In a heavy-bottomed saucepan combine sugar, honey, and water. Bring to a boil and continue to gently boil until a candy thermometer reaches 300 degrees or until a small amount of the mixture dropped into cold water forms a hard ball.

2 Fill a shallow bowl with water and ice and bring to the table.

3 Peel and slice bananas about 1-inch thick and bring to the table. Then just before serving, bring the sugar mixture to the table (use a hot pad as the pan should be very hot).

4 Using metal skewers, spear each banana chunk individually and dip into the sugar mixture, swirling to coat. Then plunge into the ice water. The sugar coating will firm and crackle. Repeat until all the banana slices are used.

NOTE *Timing makes this dish a bit tricky. The sugar mixture must remain very hot. If you have an electric fondue pot or chafing dish, pour the mixture into that to keep it warm.*
  You may enjoy dipping the bananas into the hot sugar mixture, then into toasted sesame seeds for a crunchy coating, and finally into the ice water. This recipe can be done with apple cubes as well.

CHAPTER

15

As trendy as food may become, there are some dishes that are never out of fashion. These are foods that are nourishing, uncomplicated, and always satisfying, Yet, because they aren't noteworthy, you may not have thought of making them.

Some of these, such as the Sausage-Based Chili, Baked Chicken or Meat Sauce, are variations on standards. And while the dishes may date back to your mother's cookbook, the ones that follow are more robustly seasoned. These recipes will become part of your daily repertoire.

Other recipes, like the Waldorf Salad or Salami and Eggs, are included in this chapter because they are quick and effortless.

Unlike in the other chapters, the recipes here aren't matched to make complete meals. Salade Nicoise, Lettuce, Bacon, and Blue Cheese Salad, and Potato Frittata don't need an accompaniment, though one of the breads featured elsewhere in the book would be fine.

You no doubt have your own ideas about what enhances a fiery bowl of chili, or how to round out an entree of meat sauce on fresh fettuccini.

SOME CLASSIC DISHES

WATERCRESS-SCALLOP SOUP

INGREDIENTS

2 tablespoons butter
2 leeks
1 cup firmly packed
    watercress leaves and small
    stems
³/₄ cup fish stock or clam
    juice, divided
¼ pound bay scallops,
    halved if desired

½ cup plain yogurt or
    buttermilk
Dash of fresh lemon juice
Salt and freshly ground white
    pepper to taste

1 Melt the butter in a medium pot. Trim the leeks and discard green parts. Then cut each leek lengthwise in 2. Thoroughly wash leeks. Pat dry and finely chop. Sauté leeks in butter, over low heat, covered, for 10 minutes.

2 Meanwhile, blanch watercress. Place in a large sieve and drop into boiling water for 30 seconds. Then place under cold running water to stop the cooking. Add to the leeks. Sauté 5 more minutes over low heat. Cool slightly.

3 Combine leeks, watercress, and ¼ cup fish stock or clam juice in a blender or food processor fitted with a steel blade. Puree.

4 Return the mixture to the pot. Add remaining ½ cup fish stock or clam juice and bring to a boil. Reduce heat to low and simmer 5 minutes. Add scallops and any liquid in the container to the pot. Cover and remove from heat. Let stand 5 minutes. The scallops should cook through from the heat of the fish stock. If not, simmer 2 or 3 minutes. Cool thoroughly. Stir in yogurt, lemon juice, salt, and pepper. Chill 2 or 3 hours.

TOMATO-CHEESE SOUFFLÉ

INGREDIENTS

2 medium-large, fully ripe
   tomatoes
4 tablespoons butter
4 tablespoons all-purpose
   flour
1 cup hot milk
Salt and freshly ground white
   pepper to taste

½ cup freshly grated
   Parmesan cheese
4 eggs, separated

1 Preheat oven to 350 degrees.

2 Drop tomatoes into boiling water for 30 seconds. Lift out and peel off skins. Cut each tomato in half crosswise and seed. Set cut-side down on a plate to drain off all excess liquid. It is essential that the tomatoes not be wet. Cut into small dice to yield 1 cup (save any remainders for a sauce). Set aside.

3 Melt butter in small pot. Add flour and blend well over low heat. Add milk gradually, stirring constantly until thick and smooth. Stir in salt, pepper, and cheese, stirring until cheese is blended in.

4 Beat egg yolks together in a small bowl. Spoon some of the cheese sauce into the egg yolks to raise the temperature, then spoon the egg yolk mixture into the sauce whisking constantly. Stir in tomato pieces. Pour into a large bowl and set aside.

5 In a clean, fat-free bowl beat egg whites until stiff, but not dry. Take a scoop of egg whites and stir into the yolk mixture to lighten. Fold the remaining whites into the yolk mixture, gently, and fast, but thoroughly.

6 Spoon into a buttered and floured 1½-quart soufflé dish. Bake for 40 minutes or until soufflé is firm when jiggled. Serve immediately.

SERVES 2 TO 3

SALAMI AND EGGS

INGREDIENTS

2 tablespoons olive oil
½ teaspoon cumin seed
½ cup minced onions
2 eggs
½ cup diced salami
1 tablespoon minced parsley
Salt and freshly ground black
   pepper to taste

1 Heat oil in a medium-size skillet. Add cumin and minced onions. Sauté over medium heat for 5 minutes, until onions are tender.

2 Beat eggs together and stir in salami. Pour over onions in skillet. Gently scramble over medium heat for 5 minutes, until eggs are done, but not dry. Sprinkle with parsley and salt and pepper. Toss gently. Serve immediately.

SERVES 1

POTATO FRITTATA

INGREDIENTS

2 to 4 tablespoons vegetable
  or light olive oil
1 large potato, peeled and
  thinly sliced
1 small tomato, cored,
  peeled, seeded, and
  chopped
1 clove garlic, finely minced
4 eggs

Salt and freshly ground white
  pepper to taste
2 tablespoons finely minced
  scallions
A few fresh marjoram leaves
  or a pinch of dried
  marjoram

1 Heat 2 tablespoons oil in a medium-size skillet. Add potato slices and sauté over low heat until browned on one side. Turn over and continue cooking until lightly browned on the second side, about 10 minutes in all.

2 Add tomato and garlic and cook until tomato is slightly pulpy, about 5 minutes, but do not let the garlic brown.

3 Check skillet. If vegetables have absorbed all the oil, add the remaining 2 tablespoons oil to the bottom of the skillet and heat. It is important that the eggs not stick to the skillet when they are added.

4 Beat the eggs with salt and pepper. Add the scallions. Pour into the skillet, over the vegetables. Add marjoram. Cook over medium heat until eggs are firm on underside and just firming up on top, about 5 minutes. Place a large platter over the eggs. Flip eggs onto the platter, then ease back into the skillet.

5 Either finish the eggs by placing in a preheated broiler for 1 to 2 minutes (the popular way to prepare a frittata) or return to the top of the stove and cook the top side. Cut into wedges or in half and serve immediately.

GNOCCHI WITH BACON OR HAM

INGREDIENTS

6 small new potatoes
1 egg yolk
4 to 5 level tablespoons
  all-purpose flour
¾ cup freshly grated
  Parmesan cheese
2½ tablespoons melted butter

Freshly ground white pepper
  to taste
1 teaspoon salt
8 thin slices Canadian bacon
  or prosciutto, cut into
  bite-size pieces

1 Wash potatoes and place in a small pot with water to cover. Bring to a boil, reduce heat to medium, and boil gently until potatoes are fork tender, about 15 minutes. Drain off all water.

2 Set aside to cool slightly, then peel. Mash with a potato masher. Do not use food processor or potatoes will become pasty.

3 Blend in egg yolk, 4 tablespoons flour, ½ cup Parmesan, and ½ tablespoon melted butter. Season with pepper. If mixture is too wet to be handled, add a tablespoon more flour. The dough should be soft, but dry enough to touch.

4 To form gnocchi, tear off pecan-sized pieces and roll off a fork to form the characteristic line designs on each gnocchi.

5 Bring 2 quarts water to boiling. Add salt. When water reaches a rapid boil, pour in the gnocchi and stir once. When gnocchi float to the surface, in about 2 or 3 minutes, test one. Gnocchi should be tender, not gummy. Cook another few minutes if necessary. Then remove with a slotted spoon and set aside to drain.

6 Preheat oven to 350 degrees.

7 Layer half the gnocchi in a 1½-quart ovenproof casserole. Top with 1 tablespoon melted butter. Layer on half the Canadian bacon or prosciutto. Repeat layers. Sprinkle on remaining ¼ cup Parmesan. Bake gnocchi for 30 minutes or until cheese melts and gnocchi are heated through.

NOTE *Serve this dish as a filling entree with a salad on the side.*

WALDORF SALAD

INGREDIENTS

1 medium Delicious apple
½ teaspoon lemon juice
1 celery stalk, trimmed and
  sliced into ½-inch-thick
  slices
2 tablespoons coarsely
  chopped walnuts
2 tablespoons raisins
4 tablespoons mayonnaise
1 tablespoon plain yogurt
Lettuce leaves

1 Cut apple in half and remove core. Cut apple halves into ½-inch chunks and place in a serving bowl. Toss with lemon juice. Add celery, walnuts, and raisins.

2 Add mayonnaise and yogurt and mix gently, but well.

3 Line 2 salad plates with lettuce leaves and divide mixture between the plates.

SALAD NICOISE

INGREDIENTS

4 romaine lettuce leaves,
   washed and pat dry
1 small to medium-size
   potato
4 ounces green beans
1 can (about 3½ ounces)
   tuna
1 medium-size tomato
1 tablespoon lemon juice

3 tablespoons olive oil
Salt and freshly ground black
   pepper to taste
1 heaping tablespoon capers
1½ teaspoons fresh, minced
   basil

1 Trim tough ends off romaine. Arrange leaves on large, flat salad plate. Set aside.

2 Bring a small pot of water to the boil. Add potato and cook until tender, about 20 to 25 minutes. Drain. When cool enough to handle, peel and slice. Arrange on one quarter of the lettuce-lined plate.

3 While potato is cooking, trim green beans and cut into 1-inch lengths. Steam for 10 minutes, or until tender. Arrange on second quarter of the plate.

4 Drain tuna and arrange on the third section.

5 Then dice tomato (if desired, peel and seed first) and arrange on remaining quarter.

6 Whisk together lemon juice and olive oil. Season with salt and pepper. Drizzle over salad. Sprinkle with capers and basil.

SERVES 1

LETTUCE, BACON, AND BLUE CHEESE SALAD

INGREDIENTS

2 strips bacon
3 tablespoons light olive oil
2 to 3 teaspoons lemon juice
Salt and freshly ground white
    pepper to taste
2 cups torn Bibb or Boston
    lettuce, washed and dried
4 tablespoons crumbled blue
    cheese

1 In a small skillet, fry bacon until crisp. Drain on paper towels and crumble. Set aside.

2 Whisk together oil, lemon juice, salt, and pepper. Toss together lettuce, cheese, and bacon in a salad bowl.

3 Pour in dressing just before serving.

SERVES 2 AS A SALAD COURSE; 1 AS AN ENTREE

NOTE *This is a basic salad that can be enhanced in numerous ways. Substitute nutritious spinach for the lettuce. Add ½ cup of cooked garbanzo beans, ¼ cup chopped walnuts, a handful of sprouts to the salad.*

DUCK AND ORANGE SALAD

INGREDIENTS

1 duck (4½ pounds)
Salt and freshly ground black
* pepper to taste*
1 medium seedless orange
1 small red onion
¼ packed cup Italian parsley,
* minced*

2 tablespoons balsamic or
* red-wine vinegar*
4 tablespoons oil (half olive
* oil and half vegetable oil is*
* preferable)*
½ tablespoon light soy sauce
Lettuce leaves

1 Preheat oven to 450 degrees.

2 Remove giblets and liver from duck cavity (freeze and save for meat sauce). Rinse duck with water and pat dry. Salt and pepper the inside of the cavity. Place duck, breast-side up on a rack in a shallow roasting pan. (The rack is essential to keep the duck from cooking in a pool of melted fat.) Roast for 1 hour, pouring off any accumulated fat occasionally.

3 Remove duck from oven and allow to cool until it can be handled.

4 Peel off skin. Tear into bite-size pieces and measure ½ cup. Place the skin in a heavy-bottomed skillet. Cook over low heat about ten minutes, until thin and crisp. Remove duck skin and set aside. It will become more crisp as it cools. Discard the fat in the skillet or strain it through a sieve into a jar and refrigerate to use later as cooking fat.

5 Cut the duck from the carcass and tear into bite-size pieces. Place in a salad bowl. Peel orange and cut into bite-size pieces. Combine with the duck. Peel onion and slice paper thin. Cut each slice into half circles. Add to the duck with the parsley. Whisk together vinegar, oil, soy sauce, and pepper. Taste and add salt if necessary. Pour over duck salad and toss well.

6 Line 2 plates with lettuce and arrange duck over the greens. Sprinkle duck cracklings over the duck. Serve immediately.

DEEP-FRIED CATFISH

INGREDIENTS

¾ pound catfish
1 cup plus 6 tablespoons milk
Oil for deep-fat frying
6 tablespoons self-rising flour
(see note)
¼ cup cornmeal
1 egg
Freshly ground white pepper
to taste

Salt to taste
Chestnut Street Grill's Tartar
Sauce (page 75)

1 Cut catfish into 1- to 1½-inch cubes. Soak in 1 cup of milk for 30 minutes. Drain and set aside.

2 Preheat 1½ to 2 inches vegetable oil to 375 degrees in a heavy-bottomed skillet.

3 While oil is heating, whisk together self-rising flour, cornmeal, egg, and remaining 6 tablespoons milk. Add pepper.

4 Drop the catfish cubes into the batter, a few at a time, allowing excess batter to drip off. Ease 4 or 5 cubes at a time into hot oil. Don't crowd. When cubes are well-browned on one side, about 3 to 5 minutes, turn over and brown the remaining side. Remove and drain on paper towels while frying the remaining catfish. Divide between 2 plates and season with salt. Serve with the Chestnut Street Grill's Tartar sauce.

NOTE *Self-rising flour contains salt and baking powder, so no additional salt is necessary in the batter. If substituting regular for self-rising flour add ½ teaspoon baking powder and ⅛ teaspoon salt to the 6 tablespoons all-purpose flour.*

BAKED CHICKEN

INGREDIENTS

2 tablespoons unsalted butter
2 teaspoons mustard
4 tablespoons freshly grated
    Parmesan cheese
4 tablespoons freshly made
    bread crumbs
Freshly ground white pepper
    to taste
2 chicken thighs or breast
    halves

1 Preheat oven to 375 degrees.

2 In a medium skillet melt butter. Add mustard and stir to combine. Set aside. On a dinner plate, stir together Parmesan cheese, bread crumbs, and white pepper.

3 Place the chicken pieces in the butter mixture, turning to coat both sides. Roll in bread-crumb mixture, pressing crumbs into chicken with fingers.

4 Grease a piece of foil and place on a cookie sheet. Place chicken on greased foil and place in oven. Allow 30 to 35 minutes for thighs; 40 to 45 minutes for breast halves.

NOTE *Recipe can be halved.*

CHUTNEY CHICKEN

INGREDIENTS

1 large clove garlic
½-inch piece of gingerroot
½ tablespoon butter
2 chicken breast halves
¼ cup Major Grey's chutney
   (see note)

¼ cup plum or other
   semisweet white wine
Salt and freshly ground white
   pepper to taste

1 Preheat oven to 400 degrees.

2 Mince together the garlic and ginger. Melt butter in a small saucepan and sauté ginger and garlic for 5 minutes. Be careful that the ingredients don't burn.

3 Make a deep slash in the thick part of each chicken breast half. Divide ginger-garlic mixture between each chicken pocket. Place chicken on foil-lined cookie sheet.

4 Combine chutney and wine in a small saucepan. Cook over medium heat 5 minutes, until mixture is thickened and syrupy. Pour over the chicken. Bake for 30 to 40 minutes, basting occasionally with pan juices. Season with salt and pepper. Serve hot or tepid.

NOTE *Major Grey's chutney is made by several companies and is available in gourmet sections of grocery stores and in Indian food stores. Choose the brand that suits your tastes. Another fruit chutney can be substituted.*
   You may find the ginger-garlic a little overpowering. It flavors the chicken and can be scraped out just before serving if desired.

MINI MEAT LOAVES AND POTATOES

INGREDIENTS

½ pound ground chuck
1 clove garlic, minced
½ cup bread crumbs
2 tablespoons fresh, minced
* parsley, divided*
1 egg, lightly beaten
4 ounces tomato sauce with
* onions*
Salt and freshly ground black
* pepper to taste*

12 medium-size, pimiento-
* stuffed olives, cut in half*
* lengthwise*
4 or 5 small new potatoes
2 tablespoons butter

1 Preheat oven to 350 degrees.

2 In a large bowl combine the chuck, garlic, bread crumbs, 1 tablespoon parsley, egg, tomato sauce, salt, and pepper. Stir well, but gently.

3 Lightly oil 2 mini loaf pans, each 2½ by 4½ inches. Pack one fourth of the meat mixture into each loaf pan. Arrange a layer of sliced olives over each loaf. Spoon on remaining meat mixture and level off with the back of a spoon.

4 Bake for 30 minutes, or until meat is done and top is browned.

5 While meat loaves are baking, prepare potatoes. Wash them and place in a small pot with water to cover. Bring to a boil, reduce heat to medium, and boil gently until potatoes are fork tender, about 15 minutes. Drain off all water. Add remaining tablespoon parsley, butter, salt, and pepper to the potatoes in the pot. Cook over low heat, shaking pot frequently so butter coats the potatoes.

6 To serve, let the meat loaves stand in the pans for 5 minutes, so juices are absorbed. Then turn out onto individual plates and spoon the potatoes along side.

SAUSAGE-BASED CHILI

INGREDIENTS

½ pound hot Italian sausage
½ pound sweet Italian
sausage
1 tablespoon vegetable oil
(optional)
1 small green bell pepper,
cored and diced
1 medium onion, peeled and
chopped

1 jalapeño pepper, seeded,
rinsed and chopped
½ tablespoon chili powder
Generous dash of red pepper
flakes
1¼ cups water
1 can (6 ounces) tomato paste
Cooked rice, kidney beans,
pinto beans, or macaroni

1 Remove sausage from casings. Break into small chunks. Brown in large pot over medium heat, stirring frequently. Remove and reserve sausages.

2 If there is no fat left in the pot, add vegetable oil. Over low heat add green pepper and cook, stirring occasionally for 5 minutes, or until just tender. Add onion and cook another 5 minutes. Stir in jalapeño pepper, chili powder, red pepper flakes, reserved sausage, water, and tomato paste. Stir well.

3 Bring to a boil. Reduce heat to low and simmer, uncovered, for 1½ hours. Spoon rice, beans, or macaroni into 2 bowls and top with chili.

SERVES 4

NOTE *This chili freezes well. Pack into ½-pint containers and freeze up to 6 months.*
This is very spicy chili, and a bland starch such as the rice, beans or macaroni becomes a welcome addition to tone down the heat.

MEAT SAUCE

INGREDIENTS

½ cup chopped green pepper
2 tablespoons vegetable oil
½ cup minced onion
1 clove garlic, minced
½ pound ground chuck
1 can (15 ounces) tomato
   puree
½ teaspoon crushed, dried
   oregano

½ teaspoon fresh, minced
   thyme or ⅛ to ¼ teaspoon
   crushed, dried thyme
2 bay leaves
Dash of red pepper flakes
Salt and freshly ground black
   pepper to taste

1 In a large skillet, sauté green pepper in oil for 5 minutes. Add onion and garlic and sauté 5 minutes more. Add meat and break up with a spoon. Cook until meat is browned. Pour off any fat.

2 Add tomato puree, oregano, thyme, bay leaves, red pepper flakes, salt, and pepper. Simmer, uncovered, for 15 to 20 minutes. Remove bay leaves before serving.

NOTE *This makes enough meat sauce for 2 servings of spaghetti. The sauce can also be served over sauteed eggplant slices, spaghetti squash halves, or baked acorn squash halves.*

JAM MUFFINS

INGREDIENTS

Butter
½ cup all-purpose flour
½ cup stone-ground
*   cornmeal*
2 teaspoons baking powder
¼ teaspoon salt
2 tablespoons sugar
1 egg, beaten

⅓ cup milk
2 tablespoons butter, melted
2 rounded tablespoons
*   orange marmalade*

1 Preheat oven to 350 degrees.

2 Butter 8 muffin cups to generously grease and set aside.

3 In a medium bowl, mix together all-purpose flour, cornmeal, baking powder, salt, and sugar. Stir well.

4 Combine egg, milk, and melted butter, stirring well. Pour the egg mixture into the flour mixture and stir just to moisten ingredients. Do not beat.

5 Spoon a rounded tablespoon batter into each greased muffin cup. Then add a teaspoon marmalade to each. Cover with remaining batter. Muffin cups should be filled no more than two-thirds full. If necessary, grease and fill an additional cup.

6 Bake for 20 to 25 minutes. Run a knife around each muffin cup to ease out the muffins. Wait 5 minutes, then turn out onto a wire rack.

MAKES 8 OR 9 MUFFINS

CONVERSION TABLES

The following are conversion tables and other information applicable to those converting the recipes in this book for use in other English-speaking countries. The cup and spoon measures given in this book are U.S. Customary (cup = 236 mL; 1 tablespoon = 15 mL). Use these tables when working with British Imperial or Metric kitchen utensils.

LIQUID MEASURES

The Imperial pint is larger than the U.S. pint; therefore note the following when measuring the liquid ingredients.

U.S.

1 cup = 8 fluid ounces
½ cup = 4 fluid ounces
1 tablespoon = ¾ fluid ounce

IMPERIAL

1 cup = 10 fluid ounces
½ cup = 5 fluid ounces
1 tablespoon = 1 fluid ounce

U.S. MEASURE	METRIC*	IMPERIAL*
1 quart (4 cups)	*950 mL*	*1½ pints + 4 tablespoons*
1 pint (2 cups)	*450 mL*	*¾ pint*
1 cup	*236 mL*	*¼ pint + 6 tablespoons*
1 tablespoon	*15 mL*	*1 + tablespoon*
1 teaspoon	*5 mL*	*1 teaspoon*

SOLID MEASURES

Outside the U.S., cooks measure more items by weight. Here are approximate equivalents for basic items in this book.*

* So as to avoid awkward measurements, some conversions are not exact.

	U.S. CUSTOMARY	METRIC	IMPERIAL
Apples (peeled and chopped)	2 cups	225 g	8 ounces
Beans (dried, raw)	1 cup	225 g	8 ounces
Butter	1 cup	225 g	8 ounces
	1/2 cup	115 g	4 ounces
	1/4 cup	60 g	2 ounces
	1 tablespoon	15 g	1/2 ounce
Cheese (grated)	1 cup	115 g	4 ounces
Chocolate chips	1/2 cup	85 g	3 ounces
Coconut (shredded)	1/2 cup	60 g	2 ounces
Fruit (chopped)	1 cup	225 g	8 ounces
Herbs (chopped)	1/4 cup	7 g	1/4 ounce
Meats/Chicken (chopped, cooked)	1 cup	175 g	6 ounces
Mushrooms (chopped)	1 cup	70 g	2 1/2 ounces
Nut Meats (chopped)	1 cup	115 g	4 ounces
Pasta (dried, raw)	1 cup	225 g	8 ounces
Peas (shelled)	1 cup	225 g	8 ounces
Potatoes (mashed)	2 cups	450 g	1 pound
Raisins (and other dried fruits)	1 cup	175 g	6 ounces
Rice (uncooked)	1 cup	225 g	8 ounces
(cooked)	3 cups	225 g	8 ounces
Spinach (cooked)	1/2 cup	285 g	10 ounces
Vegetables (chopped, raw: onions, celery)	1 cup	115 g	4 ounces

* Note that exact quantities are not always given. Differences are more crucial when dealing with larger quantities. For teaspoon and tablespoon measures, simply use scant or generous quantities; or for more accurate conversions, rely upon metric.

DRY MEASURES

The following items are measured by weight outside of the U.S. These items are variable, especially the flour, depending on individual variety of flour and moisture. American cup measurements on following items are loosely packed; flour is measured directly from package (presifted).

	U.S. CUSTOMARY	METRIC	IMPERIAL
Flour (all-purpose or plain)	1 cup	150 g	5 ounces
	½ cup	70 g	2½ ounces
(bread or strong) (cake)	1 cup	125 g	4¼ ounces
Cornmeal	1 cup	175 g	6 ounces
Bran	1 cup	60 g	2 ounces
Wheat Germ	1 cup	85 g	3 ounces
Rolled Oats (raw)	1 cup	115 g	4 ounces
Sugar (granulated or caster)	1 cup	190 g	6½ ounces
	½ cup	85 g	3 ounces
	¼ cup	40 g	1¾ ounces
(confectioners' or icing)	1 cup	80 g	2⅔ ounces
	½ cup	40 g	1⅓ ounces
	¼ cup	20 g	¾ ounce
(soft brown)	1 cup	160 g	5⅓ ounces
	½ cup	80 g	2⅔ ounces
	¼ cup	40 g	1⅓ ounces

OVEN TEMPERATURES

Gas Mark	¼	2	4	6	8
Fahrenheit	225	300	350	400	450
Celsius	110	150	180	200	230

INDEX